A Father's Love

By Edna Stark

Orange Hat Publishing
www.orangehatpublishing.com - Waukesha, WI

A Father's Love
Copyrighted © 2019 by Edna Stark
ISBN 978-1-64538-041-2
First Edition

A Father's Love
By Edna Stark
Cover Design by Kaeley Dunteman

For information, please contact:

Orange Hat Publishing
www.orangehatpublishing.com
Waukesha, WI

www.orangehatpublishing.com

Dedication

I would like to dedicate my book to my four wonderful children who have been my whole life. They have been there every step of the way for me since their dad passed in 1996. I am very proud of them all. They are Kenneth, Donald, Rosemary, and Karen.

Watching them grow from babies to toddlers, and then wow! Into teenagers, and finally young men and women. It's a great gift from god.

I would also like to dedicate this book to all young men and boys who need Christian support and the love of a good family.

We pray that they will know that God will always walk alongside them, no matter where they travel. Also, to my dear friend Mary Stacy and my daughter Rosemary who helped me with the typing.

A Father's Love

Peter had continued his ministry in Rome, GA, and George Jr. kept the boys school running with the help of John, Jerry, and his Grandma Watkins. Grandma Watkins felt close to her husband George while she was working there, by keeping the memory of him alive. Grandma Watkins missed him very much, and adopting Peter was her greatest gift and treasure that God could have ever given her. Peter brought them so much joy and happiness. Now that George Sr. was gone, she had to focus on the school. She enjoyed going and talking to the boys, and knowing that her grandson was there. She knew that the boys would learn a lot about God, and how he could help them when in trouble.

Georgie graduated from college as a coach, and coached the Christian boys school team, and Lynda depended upon him a lot now that Peter was talking about leaving Georgia to go to Louisiana to help another church get back their faith in God, and they needed someone to lead them to God and to help bring the people back to them. When Peter met at his church, the committee announced to him that they need someone to take over a church in Louisiana that has had some hard times and they need a strong person to help the church get back on its feet, and also help the people, so, we thought of you Peter, rather the Bishop suggested you.

Peter expressed a great sigh, and was quiet for a few minutes. "Peter, would you and Cindy consider this move?"

"That's an awful big move to make," Peter replied.

"We understand your feelings, Peter, but you have been a wonderful leader here, and we have thought about this for a long time. And we were wondering if you would be the one to help them out."

"When would you need to know?" asked Peter. He looked very bewildered.

"Well," the committee said, "we can give you a month to decide because we need to let the

Bishop know so they can send us another Pastor for our church. So you and your family talk it over, and we will wait for your answer, okay?"

This was a surprise for Peter, and he thanked them and said, "I will talk it over with the family and give you my answer as soon as I can. And I do appreciate the offer, thank you." The committee shook hands with Peter, and would await his answer.

Cindy had been teaching Bible classes to the adults in the church and had gotten to know many people. She had come a long way from the time she was in college and met Peter. He was the only one who could show her how to trust in God, and he had helped her to trust other people too. Now, since her mother was gone, she depended on Lynda and Peter to help her raise the twins, who were grown children now.

Peter had a large decision to make. How would Cindy and Lynda take it? And Georgie who has become a young man and has taken over his grandfather's school for the boys? What would he think of his Dad leaving? What would his mother Watkins want him to do? There are so many questions to be answered. On his way home, he was quiet, and had prayed and asked

God what he would have him do.

Hope was now a music teacher in Alabama and was always wishing that her Mom and Dad could be closer to her so she could see them more. She got home maybe once a month to see them on the holidays, and always dreaded going back home to Alabama and leaving her Mom, Dad, and family. Those were special days for them. One day, she got a call from her Dad to come home for the weekend. She was glad to hear his voice.

"What's wrong, Dad?" she asked. "You sound like there is something important going on."

"There is," Peter replied, "but I need you to come home to discuss it with the whole family. Can you come?"

It was Thursday and the weekend was coming up. "Of course I will be there, Dad," Hope said. "I will leave home Friday night so the traffic won't be so heavy."

"Thank you, Hope" Peter said, "I miss you, sweetie."

"I miss you too, Dad," Hope replied. "See you Saturday afternoon. I love you."

"I love you too, Hope" said Peter, "I will see you Saturday. Drive safe."

As Peter waited for Cindy to come home, he called his mother and his son George to let them know he needed to talk to the family on Saturday and that Hope was coming home.

Lynda was surprised and asked Peter, "what is happening, Peter? Is it important?"

"Yes, Mom, it is. We will discuss it on Saturday, but I need you and Georgie to get someone to cover for you, Mom. Please let Georgie know, okay? How are you and Georgie doing?" asked Peter.

"We are doing fine, son," Lynda said. "Jerry and John are big helpers! They have grown into fine young men. Oh Peter, would it be all right if I asked them to stay with the boys on Saturday? I think they will do fine. Jerry and John have been a part of the school since they were young boys. They have learned to trust people now, and have become a part of God's family. When he was a boy at school, John ran away because he thought that no one cared about him and his parents didn't want him home because he would be in the way. Since then, John has finished High School and College, and now he has become the pride and joy of the town, helping where he can and working at the boys school along with Jerry. They have become best friends and they work together like brothers."

"Mom! That's a great idea. They have been there a while now, and they know what to do. I think they will be honored to do it," Peter answered. "I will see you this weekend, Mom, I love you." As he hung up the phone, Cindy walked in.

"Hi Peter," she said with a smile and a hug. "How was your day? Mine was delightful. We had a new family join our study today, and a young couple, and I think that they plan on getting married, and I really hope they will stay with the class. Well, I better stop talking and let you tell me about your day," as she looked at Peter wondering why he looked so sad, like he had something to say but didn't know how to say it.

She looked at Peter, and asked "Peter what is wrong? You are so quiet, what is it honey?" she asked.

Peter looked up at her and gave her a hug for comfort, and led her to where they sat in front of the fireplace. He took the bible and read, 'Where you shall go, I will follow' to Cindy.

"What does that mean, Peter?" asked Cindy.

"Remember when Jesus sent his disciples out to teach his word, and he told them wherever they go, he would be there also?" asked Peter.

"Yes, dear, what are you trying to say?" replied Cindy.

"Well, Cindy" he said, "we are having a family gathering Saturday to discuss a situation from the church committee, and Hope will be home for it."

"What situation, Peter," asked Cindy, "Is there something wrong? What does the Church committee want to do?"

Peter paused and looked at Cindy, and asked her to trust him, and that he would tell her when all the family is together.

Cindy knew that Peter had his reasons for not telling her until the whole family was together, so she didn't push it any further. They sat together by the fire quietly without any more talk. Whatever it was, God would help Peter.

When they finished reading their Bible and enjoying the warmth of the fire, they said goodnight to each other, and were looking forward to seeing Hope on Saturday.

The next morning, they woke up with the sun coming through the window. It was beautiful and shining so bright that it made them think of what a beautiful day it was going to be. Cindy went and made the coffee and breakfast while Peter showered and got ready for the family meeting. After everyone was done, Peter and Cindy said, "I wish she lived closer so we could see her more often. Georgie will be glad to see her also." Peter was deep in thought and didn't hear a word that Cindy said.

"What did you say, dear?" he asked. Cindy repeated her words to Peter. "You may get your wish, dear," he said.

"What do you mean, Peter" Cindy asked.

Peter wanted to tell her but said, "you will know shortly, okay?" He took her in his arms and held her, and kissed her softly. Cindy settled for that and waited until Peter was ready to tell everyone.

Georgie still lived at home with his Dad, but wasn't home much because he coached basketball and was the head of the Christian School that his grandpa started. He wanted to keep his promise to him no matter what - his school came first. Jerry and John agreed to work on Saturday. They had remembered how much Peter and Mrs. Watkins had done for them.

"Thank you so much boys," said Lynda. "If there's any problem, be sure to call us at Peter's home alright?"

The boys agreed and said, "everything will

be fine, Mrs. Watkins. We would like to do the weekend so you will have a couple days off, if that's alright?"

"That's great, are you sure you want to do this," she asked?

"We would love to" they answered. They knew what to do because Peter had taught them well when he was running the school with his Dad, Mr. Watkins.

Lynda and Georgie were happy about that and told Peter. She also was glad because she could spend more time with her granddaughter Hope. They haven't spent a weekend all together for a long time and this will be great. George was excited about seeing his twin sister Hope. He hadn't seen her since the beginning of school, and they had always done everything together when they were younger. He was always making sure that she was safe and no one picked on her or made fun of her because she couldn't have things to eat that other children could. She would have to be on her vegetarian diet all of her life which she has accepted and is doing good so far. George Jr. wondered if she would ever be healed, or if it is God's will of what she could show others; that it's not a handicap, but just plain sense of eating right with the help of healthy foods.

Two o'clock on Saturday, Hope drove in the driveway and her grandmother and brother George drove in just before her and greeted each other with a hug and were glad to see each other.

"What do you think Dad wants to talk to us about, Grandma?" Hope asked.

George Jr. and Lynda answered the best way they knew how. "We don't know Hope," said George, "but I guess we are all going to know soon."

"I hope it's nothing serious," said Grandma.

As they walked into the house, Peter and Cindy greeted Hope with open arms and gave Peter's Mom and George a hug.

"So glad to see you all," they said, "Come on in."

"Dad and Mom, what is this meeting all about? Is someone getting married or are we going to have a new member of the family?" asked Hope.

Hope was kidding, but thought it would be great to have a little one running around.

"Oh no!" Cindy said.

"I think those days are over for Peter and I until George and you make us grandparents. Peter will tell us soon, right Peter?" she asked.

"Dear, let's gather by the fireplace and have a little prayer."

So, they all gathered by the fire and talked about Hope's trip down and how Grandma Watkins was doing.

"Grandma, how is the school doing? George, are you still coaching?" Hope had all kinds of questions because it had been a while since she had seen them, but she was more concerned about what her Dad needed them all for. What was so important she had wondered, as she was about to find out when Peter asked them all to take hands as they prayed.

After the prayer was over, George and Hope said, "Okay, Dad, what is this all about? We are very curious."

"I don't know where to start," said Peter as he looked at his wife, Cindy, and then at Lynda.

"I...had a meeting with the church committee last week."

"About what, son?" said Lynda.

"Yeah Peter, about what?" asked Cindy.

"Well," said Peter, "this is going to be a difficult question to ask all of you," he said. "I have been thinking about how I would tell you."

"Whatever it is dear, we will try to understand

it, so you can tell us as we are all here for you."

Hope and George looked at each other trying to figure out what it could be, and would it be sad or happy for their Dad and Mom. Peter stood up and looked at his Mom and said, "Mother, you have been there for me ever since I was found on the streets, lost and hungry, but now I am lost for words, so, I guess I will just say what I have to, okay?"

"Last week, the committee at the church asked if I would take a position at the new church."

"Peter, why?" Asked Lynda and Cindy.

"Where is the church, Dad?" the twins asked him.

Peter answered Lynda and said, "The Bishop asked the committee if they would ask me to help this little church because it is in deep trouble and it needs a strong relationship. They suggested that I would be perfect for it."

"But Dad, where is this church?" they asked.

"Well," he said "what would you think of Cindy and I moving to Louisiana? Shreveport?"

"What?" They all said. "Why there?"

Georgie and Lynda were very surprised.

"Dad," replied Georgie, "does this mean that you would need to sell the house?"

Lynda remembered when Peter's Dad and she had given the house to Peter and Cindy for their wedding gift. "Peter do you have to sell the house? It's a very special place you know," asked his mother.

"I have to see if the church will find a place for us, or if there is a parsonage there, until we can find a place to live Mom."

"I don't want to sell it," Peter replied.

"All of our memories are here, Dad. It will never be home anywhere else. George and I were born and raised here," said Hope.

"We could always come home to it, please, don't sell it."

"Cindy, I haven't heard anything from you, what are your feelings on this subject?" Peter asked her. "You have been very quiet dear."

"Well, you are my husband and wherever they send you, I shall follow as God has a need of us somewhere else. Remember Peter, when you were lost and sick in the hospital, after your mother, Mrs. Gleinnis died? You quoted the verse, 'love thy neighbor as ourselves.' So, wherever you go, I will be by your side and together, we along with our faith and God's help, we will meet new friends and neighbors to share our help in Louisiana. Rome, Georgia will always be our home someday, we will be back."

"George, son, what do you have to say? Would you and Grandma like to move into the house if we can work it out? You have been a big help for Grandma and I know Grandma is proud of you."

"Grandma, what do you think?" asked George. "Will you be okay if Dad and Mom move? Maybe Hope can get a teaching job here and we can help keep the christian school running."

"Hope, will you think about it? Then we could all go and see Mom and Dad together, that would be a good vacation trip. Don't you think so, Dad?"

"I think that's a great idea, but it has to be up to all three of you and let me know what you would like to do, alright?"

Hope didn't know what to say, as she pondered over the idea of changing her schools and moving back home.

"Dad, Georgie, can I think about it?" Hope asked. "I would have to finish the year out in Alabama and check out the schools in Rome before I can say definitely yes or no."

"Well, that would be up to you Hope darling,

it's a big decision to make," Peter told her, "just as it is for your Mom and I. We will miss all of you so much but I must do what God asks me. So, you see, it's not my will but God's will."

Lynda said, "George and I will be fine and we would love to move into your house, as it was meant for the family and we don't want to leave it."

"Mom, are you alright with running the Chrisitan school? You and Georgie do very good, and Jerry and John are there also to help you if you need time out."

"Son, I know I am not getting any younger, but this is your Dad's dream, and nothing is going to keep me from holding on to it. God will watch over me and George. So, you do what you have to do, you and Cindy, alright? George will always let you know if there is anything happening, won't you George?"

"Sure will Dad, everything will be okay. We have friends here and will let you know how things go. So, don't let that worry you and Mom, just let us hear from you often and we will do the same, won't we Grandma?" George asked.

For Hope, it was about the same distance from where she lived now to where her Mom and Dad were moving to, so she had to think about what

George, her twin brother, wanted her to do. Was it because he wanted her closer so she could look after Grandma and keep her company? Could she find a teaching job there? She was good at what she does, maybe she could teach the Sunday school class. She enjoyed working with the children, she grew up with lots of children there, so she should know them and she could see her old friends again. It would be fun teaching children music and singing in church again like she did when she was home. Hope is a very intelligent girl in spite of what she has to live with, but she would have to think about all this before she could give George an answer.

"Well," said Cindy, "tomorrow is a church day, so let's all spend it together before Hope has to go back to school but right now, I think it's time for dinner. Is anyone hungry?"

"You bet we are," George said.

"I am too," said Hope.

Grandma, Peter, and the family gathered around the table, they said their blessings and enjoyed a delicious dinner. After dinner, they were all visiting with Hope and asked her how she was doing with her diet.

"I'm doing alright Mom, but I have a doctor's

appointment next month, so I will try to make it down a few days before that to help you and Dad pack."

"Would you like that, Hope? George and Grandma can come also. I know they will want to be here."

Hope looked at them and Lynda said, "We sure do! Right now, I think Georgie and I will head home and we will meet you at church tomorrow."

Georgie said, "Hope, I will see you before you leave tomorrow and we can go out for lunch or just go visit the Chrisitan school, whatever you want to do okay?"

"That sounds fine George," Hope said, "but I have to leave shortly after church, so the traffic isn't terrible, and I have some papers to do when I get back."

Georgie and Lynda said goodbye to his Dad. George had been staying with his Grandma to keep her company at night.

They waved goodbye and said, "we will see you tomorrow."

They left to go home and Lynda asked Georgie if he thought they should stop at the school.

"No, Grams, the boys are fine, they will call if

they need us, okay? So, please, don't worry. You need this time out to spend with Dad and Mom and also Hope."

Lynda said okay and felt better, and was glad to get home, but she couldn't help feeling sad that her only son was moving miles away and she wouldn't see him for awhile. Peter was always there when she needed him, just like she was for him when he was a little boy.

Lynda said, "George, how are we ever going to get used to your Mom and Dad not being here and sitting next to them in church and doing things together?"

"We have a whole month, Grandma, to get used to it. You taught me that when God calls us, we must do what he asks of us. They will be back soon as they can get the church back on its feet."

"Grandma, do you think that Hope will consider coming back home and staying with us?"

"I don't know, but it would be just wonderful to have both of my grandchildren home. Maybe she can find a music teacher's job here and help at Sunday school. Wouldn't it be nice?"

"Yes, it would be very nice," said Georgie.

They sat very quietly, and then Lynda said, "Georgie, I am going to go to bed, I am so tired and it's been a long day. So, goodnight and get a good night's sleep."

"Goodnight Grams," and he gave her a big hug.

"I am going to read for awhile," he said.

"Okay, I will see you in the morning," said Lynda.

Meanwhile, Peter was too busy to think about being tired as he and Cindy were trying to figure out who was going to move or transport the furniture, and who the new pastor was going to be here in Rome. Was his Mom going to be alright with George? He had a lot of things to talk about, and lots of people to see before they could leave.

As they sat and talked, they watched the sunset. "How beautiful the sunset is," Cindy said to Hope and Peter, who were enjoying it also.

"It's beautiful," replied Hope.

Peter turned to his daughter and asked, "Hope, would you play a couple songs for your mother and me? And also, will you play at the church tomorrow?"

"I will be happy to," Hope replied, "but what about the regular pianist Dad?"

"I will let her know," Peter said.

Hope agreed and sat down to play "Amazing Grace" and "Peace in the Valley" as they sang three songs together. The sunset glowed with bright orange and reds, like fire in the sky.

Peter spoke up and said, "this will be one picture we will never forget, that God has painted, but I'm sure there will be many more in Shreveport also."

"Not like this one, Dad," replied Hope.

"It will always remind of this time together and to know that one day, we will return home together as God has planned for us all."

The next morning, the family gathered together at church listening to Peter's sermon about friends, families, and how much they mean to each other. Peter hadn't said anything about his leaving yet because he hadn't let the committee know. He would let them know on Monday. It was a good sermon and the congregation let him know that they heard what he was saying, that their church is your family and the people are your neighbors. After they left, Georgie took Hope out for a ride and to do lunch together. They couldn't be long because Hope needed to start home early.

He had asked Hope to come and stay with him

and Grandma. He didn't know how Lynda would be after his Dad and Mom were gone.

"Hope, did you think about coming back after the school year?" he asked.

"I think Grandma will be very lonesome when Mom and Dad leave, especially since Grandpa is gone. Please, Hope, at least think about it," said George.

"Okay, little brother, I definitely will think about it, but I will need to have you check in to some schools for me, can you and Grandma do that?" she asked. "And some job openings?"

"We will be glad to," George said.

As twins, they had always been close and would always know the other one's feelings.

"Grandma and I can watch the papers and when you come up to see your doctor, we can get some applications for you. I just feel that Grandma needs someone she can talk to besides me, someone she can go to church and shopping with," he said.

"Oh, alright, George, I will have to see how the jobs do first."

"There's always a place at the boys school for you," he said, "until you get a teaching job. We can get the boys to start a boys choir. Some of them love to sing and have very good voices, but we don't have a teacher."

"Well," said Hope, "we will see, and I must get started for home now, so let's go see the rest of the family, so I can say goodbye and you need to pick up Grandma at Mom's, okay?"

As they drove home, they were quiet until they were almost home.

"I miss having you around, Sis," said George.

"I miss you too, little brother, except we're not so little anymore, are we?"

As they reached home, Peter and his Mom and Cindy were sitting outside enjoying the fresh air and the beautiful spring flowers.

"Did you two have a nice lunch?" they asked.

"Oh yes, we certainly did," said Hope. "It's good to see the town again and see some of my old friends, but I must get ready and leave because it's a long drive home and I have to get back to work tomorrow."

Hope was still going to class at night for teaching and tutoring some students.

"Well, it has been so nice to see you darling, and we will let you know when we will be leaving, okay?" They all gave her a hug and told her that they love her.

"Drive careful," Cindy said.

As she drove away, George waved goodbye and watcher her until she was out of sight. He was sure she would be back to stay.

"Grandma, are you ready to go home?" asked Georgie.

"Yes dear," Lynda replied, "I am getting a little tired and we need to check in on Jerry and John at the school, okay?"

"We can do that Grandma," said Georgie.

They turned to Cindy and Peter and asked them to let them know when they needed help.

"We will mother," said Peter.

"And Mom," said Cindy, "we'll see you everyday until we leave, and we'll miss you very much."

Lynda gave Cindy a hug and tears came to their eyes.

"I never thought that I would lose my son and you to another church, but I know that's what God has planned for you, so you must do it. We will see you tomorrow."

Georgie embraced his father and he would miss having him and Mom around.

"Dad, grandpa would be proud of you."

"Mom," Peter asked, "would you two like to

come to the church meeting with Cindy and me? It will be tomorrow afternoon at two. If you would like to be there, then you would know what is happening and when the day will be."

"Peter, that would be wonderful," said Lynda. "It would be so nice to know what my son has to do, and meet some of the ladies on the committee." Lynda thought she could get a little active in the church while he was gone.

"Your father would like that."

"Then it's settled," Peter said. "We will meet you at the church tomorrow."

Lynda and Georgie drove home in silence, each one wondering what the other was thinking. Suddenly, Lynda spoke and asked, "Georgie, what are you thinking of? You are very quiet. Are you disappointed that your Dad is leaving?"

"No Grams, it's just that I thought he would be around forever to help with the boys, so it wouldn't be so much work for you. My coaching takes up my time, so you are alone a lot and I wish you weren't. I asked Hope to think about coming back home to teach and help you."

"Georgie, what did she say?" asked Lynda.

"Oh, here we are at the school Grams, I will tell you later. Let's go see how the boys are."

"Okay, Georgie, but we will talk later."

Lynda was curious to know what Hope had said. They entered the school and noticed that it was very quiet although it was early in the evening.

"Where is everyone?" George asked, "it is so quiet."

As they walked in, they noticed that the boys were in the Chapel with John and Jerry.

"What is happening John?" Georgie asked as they saw the boys praying and the pastor was there to console the boys.

"Yes, boys, is there something wrong," asked Lynda? They walked over to Pastor Olson and asked, what happened.

"Well," he said, "one of the boys lost his mother today. I guess she had been pretty sick with pneumonia and she passed away last night, he is very upset and doesn't want to talk to anyone."

"Who was it?" asked Lynda and George.

"Scott Weston's mother," John said. "That's why we are gathered here to say a prayer for Scott and his Dad."

"I think we better call Dad," said George, "he will want to know, don't you think so Grandma?"

"Yes, I do think he would. Jerry, would you give him a call for us?"

"Yes ma'am," Jerry answered and left to make his phone call to Peter.

Jerry returned and let them know that Peter would be right there.

"Thank you Jerry," replied Pastor Olson.

"Where is Scott," asked George, "and why isn't he with his father at a time like this?"

Pastor Olson walked over by George and mentioned that Scott's father asked if Scott could stay here tonight while he took care of things, and if he could pick Scott up in the morning.

"I know it's hard on Scott, but I think it's the best thing for him, he is with his friends."

Peter soon arrived and asked to see Scott.

"George, would you and mother please help Pastor Olson, and I will go talk to Scott. Oh, what room is he in?"

John replied, "He is in room 112."

"Thank you," said Peter, and walked over to Scott's room. He knocked softly but there was no answer, so he walked in and found Scott crying.

"Scott," said Peter softly, "are you alright?"

"I'm so sorry about your Mom, would you like to talk about it?"

Scott sat up, looked at Peter, and threw his

arms around him. Peter embraced him and held Scott for a few moments.

Then Scott said, "I don't want my Mom to leave us, we need her. Why did God have to take her? Why Mr. Watkins, why? My Dad needs her too."

He started crying again and Peter was reminded of the time that he cried for his Mom and didn't want her to go either.

"Scott, how old are you?"

"I'm going to be twelve next month, and Mommy won't be here on my birthday."

Scott started crying harder and Peter embraced him and dried his tears.

"Scott," said Peter, holding him on his lap like he had when Hope was in the hospital, "let me tell you about the time when I was twelve and I lost my father to a serious disease called Legionnaires disease. At that time, there was no cure for many illnesses. I thought that the world was going to end, but my mother Glennis got me through it, just like your father, you, and the love of God will do."

"Where is your mother," asked Scott?

"Well, my Mom and I prayed together each night. We prayed for my father at bedtime, and two years later my mother died and I was alone, hungry, and cold. But you have your Dad yet and he needs you to be strong, okay?"

"But Peter, where did you go when your mother Glennis died?" asked Scott.

"Well, Scott, God had his plans already made and a good family by the name of Mr. and Mrs. George Watkins adopted me."

"Mrs. Watkins is your mother?" asked Scott.

"Yes, and I love her very much, my second father also died but I have lots of memories of him. And they gave me a Christian upbringing and gave me lots of love and security and now, I have two grown children of my own."

"What are their names?" asked Scott, wiping the tears from his eyes.

"Well, you know them, they are George and Hope," Peter answered.

"So you see Scottie, you need to be brave tomorrow when you and your father say goodbye to your Mom. Do you think that you can do that?"

Scott looked sadly up at Peter and said, "I, I will try but why do we have to say goodbye? Someday, I might see her."

"Hmmm," Peter thought, "well not really goodbye, but if you go see her you can tell her

28

that you love her and that you will take good care of your Daddy and you will never, never forget her. Do you know what I mean Scott?"

Scott walked over to his mother's picture and said, "I guess...but Dad and I will always remember Mom!"

"Will you be there tomorrow Peter," he asked?

"I sure will," Peter replied.

"Now, do you think that you can come and thank everyone for their prayers and say goodnight to them?"

"Okay," said Scott as he wiped the tears from his eyes and walked out with Peter. Scott looked up at everyone and saw how sad they looked at him then he went over by Georgie and the boys.

"I...I... want to thank you all for praying for my Dad and I, you all have been so nice to me. So, I guess, I will say goodnight to all of you, okay?"

As he walked back to his room, he looked back at Peter and said, "I will see you tomorrow, Peter."

"Thank you Dad," said Georgie and the rest of the staff, "I don't know what we are going to do when you move away."

The boys hadn't heard that Peter was leaving

and they all stood up and said, "No Peter, don't go, please."

"Dad, I am sorry, I thought they knew," said George.

"Georgie," said his Grandma, "that's alright they have to know anyways."

"Yes, son, let me tell them, okay?"

"Alright Dad," said Georgie.

As Georgie walked over by John, Jerry, and the Pastor, Pastor asked the boys if they would please sit down as we need to talk about Mr. Watkins leaving.

"Okay," said the boys.

"Why...why is he going?" asked one of the younger boys called Nick.

"Well, Mr. Watkins will tell you, so please listen carefully."

Peter walked up by the boys and Pastor Olson, who is the Chaplain of the school. "Well, boys, you know that I am the pastor of our church in town, don't you?"

"Yes," they replied. "Well, when God calls us to help someone in need, we want to go and help, right?"

"Yes sir," the boys said.

"So there is a church in Louisiana that is having

some hard times, and they have asked for help, and the church Bishop asked me and Cindy to go and help build the church up again and bring the people in that town back together."

John and Jerry were surprised but told Peter that they will be here as long as he needed them.

To the boys it was a sad time. "Aren't you going to be with Scott this week? He really likes you," said one of them, "and he really needs you Mr. Watkins."

"Oh yes, boys, I sure will. And we will see you a lot before we leave. Also, Georgie, my son and Mrs. Watkins, my mother, will help you through any problems you have, does that sound okay?"

"Yes, Peter, but we will miss you."

"Cindy and I will miss you all very, very much but Jerry and John have been here since little boys, and know a lot and the pastor will also help whenever you need to talk. Georgie will be here for you also, so you see, you have lots of good people who care. I will always stop in when I am in town to see the family, how does that sound?"

"Great," they replied.

"Yeah, well, I think we will have Pastor Olson say a prayer and you can get ready for the night."

Pastor Olson said the prayer and Peter said

goodbye and goodnight to his Mom and Georgie.

"Well," he said, to his Mom Lynda, "I will see you tomorrow so you and Georgie have a good night, as there is a lot to do and we will see you at the meeting tomorrow."

"Alright dear," his mother said, "have a good night," and they departed to go home.

The following day, the committee and Peter met in a special gathering. Lynda, Cindy, and Georgie joined them, introducing each other to everyone trying to make it a relaxing group before they really get to say what everyone was thinking. Peter began by asking everyone to pray with him as he asked for guidance and protection for Scott Weston and his father.

The chairman of the board spoke up when Peter finished with the Prayer and asked, "Peter have you come to a decision, have you decided on taking the position in Louisiana?"

It was quiet for a minute, and then Peter looked up at his mother and son Georgie with a sad look on his face. "Well," he said, "as much as I hate to leave my family behind and we have discussed it at great lengths, I know God will always be there for them, so the family has agreed and we will be honored to accept the position."

They all smiled, and yet they were a little saddened to have to let him go.

"Peter, it will take a great man to fill your place! The church will watch over your mother and family."

"Thank you very much, that would be appreciated, do you have anyone to replace me yet?" Peter asked.

"No, not yet but the Bishop is still working on it and until we do, can you think of anyone Peter?" they asked.

Georgie interrupted and asked if he could say something, which surprised the committee and Peter.

"You sure may," they answered.

"Well Dad, you know Pastor Olson at the school, right?"

"Sure son, are you thinking he could fill in until the church finds someone?"

"Yes Dad, he has been very good with the boys and a magnificent teacher of the bible, what do you think? That's when you got your first start Dad."

The committee looked at each other and then they looked at Peter.

"Georgie may have a good idea, Peter,"

replied one of the members, "when would you be able to meet with him?" they asked.

"Well Dad, do you think it will be okay?" asked Georgie.

"If it's okay, with the rest of them, we can meet with Pastor Olson on Thursday," said Peter.

"It would be an honor to meet him, that's if you and Georgie agree that he would be good for the church, we will be glad to talk with him. Can you set it up with him?"

George and Peter visited Charles the next day and asked him if he would fill in until the Church gets a new minister. Charles met with the committee and agreed to fill in, and the staff was very pleasant.

"Things went rather smooth Cindy, didn't they?" asked Peter.

"Yes dear, it was nice of George to think about Pastor Olson. He will do well. So, when do we leave, and where are we going to stay when we get there?" she asked.

"We leave at the end of the month, and the church has a house all picked out for us dear, so we have lots of work to do."

"I would like to get mother settled here before we go," Peter said. "It will be a big move for her.

I will let Hope know, and she will come and help Mom and George, she only has a few more weeks before school is out. So Mom will be happy to have her, she has been doing great on her diet even though it's hard for her."

"Peter darling, what if we had a farewell party so we can see all of our friends and neighbors together? Would you like that?" asked Cindy.

"I think that's a swell idea," Peter said.

The weeks passed by quickly it seemed. The movers packed most of the things and Peter's Mom wrapped all the dishes after the farewell gathering. The family, Hope, Georgie, Grandma, Peter, and Cindy went to Lynda's house to help her with the move to Peter's home. Georgie felt like being home again because that's where he grew up, and if his wish came true, Hope would be home with them also and that would be an answered prayer.

The day before moving day, Peter asked his Mom (Lynda) if she would like to go with him to the cemetery to see his Dad and Cindy's Mom before they leave. His mother could still drive, but not a long distance. She didn't like the freeway with the heavy traffic and some crazy drivers, so she was happy to have Peter ask her.

"Oh son, I would like that very much, we can talk to Dad together and tell him that he won't be alone because I'll be there."

That afternoon, Peter picked up his Mom and quietly drove along when he said to his Mom, "are you going to be alright mother while I am gone? You know you can come and stay with us if you want to or even come visit us."

"Yes son, I will be fine. Hope is planning on coming home after school, and if she can find a teaching job here, then she will stay with us."

"That will be a great Mom," said Peter.

As they arrived at the cemetery, they noticed that someone else had been there. Lynda had asked Peter if he had been here earlier, and he said, "no Mom, but who ever was put some beautiful flowers on Dads grave."

Lynda had picked up a rose bush plant to put by George's stone. "Son," she asked, "would you help me plant this rose bush for your father? I thought it would bloom all summer."

"Sure Mom, let's find some dirt and a shovel."

"Oh, I have some Peter," she said.

Peter took the little shovel and dug the hole near the stone. He planted it so that it was in solid ground. He took his mother's hands and they prayed together and hoped that the roses would bloom every year until Peter and Cindy returned home. When they finished they walked over by Cindy's Mom's grave (Mary), and they sat down as they did for his Dad and they also planted a rose bush for Cindy's Mom.

"We will take good care of her Mary," Peter said. "Cindy will always think of you, and we will see you whenever we come to town to see Mother and the children and my Dad's grave, and we will always love you Mary."

As they looked at each other, they knew it was time to go home, but hated to say goodbye to both George and Mary.

The Big Move

The last week that Peter was to give his sermon, he introduced Pastor Charles Olson to the congregation. He started with a prayer and the congregation sang "Rock of Ages."

Peter said, "good morning friends and all, God is sure with us today isn't he? What I have to say many of you already know, but I will be leaving at the end of the month to answer God's call to another church that needs help getting things back on track in Shreveport, so today friends, Pastor Olson is our guest and I am letting him introduce himself to you, please welcome him."

Pastor Olson introduced himself and said, "Many of you know me as the Chaplain at the boys school. I am not married, I love working with the boys at the school, the staff there is wonderful and I live in Rome, GA. I am looking forward to being your Pastor until the Bishop finds one for you. I will be here as long as you need me. Thank you and I welcome any questions that you may have. We will now let Peter conintue this morning's sermon. Oh! There is one more thing. You are all welcome to attend a farewell party after church at the boys school in honor of Peter and Cindy.

Peter, surprised by the invitation, said, "thank you," to everyone and they sang the final song "Where he leads me, I will follow" for the closing hymn.

The congregation joined the party at the school and John and Jerry - now the staff members along with the rest of the family - called everyone's attention to the boys.

Peter said, "Pastor Olson, the boys at the school would like to say something."

Scott Weston, the boy who lost his mother recently, got up and they sang a song of farewell to Peter and Cindy. Jerry and John gave a speech, and dedicated their lives to do the best they can, along with George and Mrs. Watkins.

"We all love you Peter, and your father, who is up in heaven and would be proud of you. We will miss you very much."

Scott raised his hand and said, "Peter, we want to thank you for being here for us and we would like to present this gift to you as a remembrance of all of our love here." He looked at Peter with tears in his eyes. Peter embraced him.

"Thank you all," he said. "I will always keep in touch with you because I will need you now to take care of Grandma Watkins, okay?"

The members of the church clapped their hands and mingled amongst the dinner tables and visited with the boys and the new Pastor. As the crowd slowly left, they wished Peter and Cindy a good trip, and may God go with him and Cindy. When the room cleared, Peter and his family talked to the boys and gave them all a chance to talk to Peter alone if they wished to say goodbye to him.

As the evening ended, Peter and Cindy asked Hope, who had been very quiet at the party, if everything was okay.

"Is everything alright with you?"

"Mom, Dad, I am fine but I do need to talk to you tonight when we get home."

Cindy replied, "sure sweetheart, whatever it is."

What was it that worried her, could she be sick again? Would this move be wrong for her?

All these questions concerned Cindy, but she decided to wait until they were alone tonight.

Hope was always a fragile little girl, and yet outgoing and ambitious. She had made friends wherever she went, but she always had to watch her health more than most children. Lynda and Georgie had said goodnight to Peter and the family, then headed for home.

"See you tomorrow Dad," Georgie called out as they drove away.

When Peter and Cindy arrived at home with Hope, who was not saying much in the car, and it drew Peter's attention. Hope was now a young lady and was still their little girl and they could tell that there was something worrying her.

Peter put his arms around her and asked, "Hope, come and sit down next to me. I know there is something on your mind."

Peter and Cindy sat next to Hope while she wondered how they would feel about moving back to help Grandma and her brother with things here, but is that what she really wanted to do?

Curiously, Peter asked Hope, "What's wrong?"

Hope began to tell her parents what she was considering.

"Mom, Dad, Georgie wants me to move home with them so I can help Grandma so she won't be so lonesome. Georgie is gone a lot with his coaching at the boys school. What do you think I should do? she asked.

"Hope you have to do what you feel you should do," replied Cindy.

"It's a big decision to make, what about your job at the school? How do you feel about it?"

"Well," said Hope, "Grandma and Georgie said that I could work at the school and I could teach the boys choir until I get a teaching job. I also would be closer to my doctor."

"Oh, Hope," said Peter, "that's a great idea, Grandma would love that and I would feel much better because Grandma would have both of her grandchildren with her, she would love that since grandpa's gone. You twins mean the world to her."

"So you think it will be alright?" Hope asked.

"Darling, it would be wonderful, but it has to be your decision."

"Thanks Mom, thanks Dad, I feel like a load has been lifted and God has answered."

The following week was a busy one for everyone. Hope had decided to move home to help Grandma.

Peter and Cindy were busy getting things ready to go to their new destination. The family gathered together on the day the moves came for the big day. Many of the neighbors came to say goodbye to them. Tears were shed by all of them, especially Lynda, Peter's Mom. She was really going to miss them. The movers had left that afternoon, and the following day Peter and Cindy were getting ready to leave early, as was Hope.

"Mom," said Peter, giving her a hug and told her that he would be home before she knew it.

"We will call you as soon as we get there, okay?"

They embraced Hope and said, "I am so proud of you, and if you ever need to talk, call us," said Cindy.

Georgie gave his Mom and Dad a hug and said, "We will miss you, and we will take good care of Grandma, Dad."

As Peter and Cindy drove out of sight, Georgie and Hope took Lynda's hand and watched them until they couldn't see them anymore. Gerogie and his Grandma then walked in the house, looked around and Hope came in later.

"What an empty feeling it is, right Grandma?"

Hope's eyes began to show tears, and Lynda

took her in her arms and told her, "Hope, it's going to be alright sweetie, we will all be together again and Georgie and I will be so happy to have you here with us."

"You bet we will sis," replied Georgie. "Sis, we will help you in any way we can because we want you to stay, so what can we do?"

"Well how would you like to drive with me back to Alabama to get my things at the apartment next weekend? I could use some company and help," she replied.

"Moving back home where we were raised will be a comfort to us," Georgie and Lynda agreed.

"It will be a pleasure Hope to help you and get to see the scenery along the way. Georgie and I would be glad to do it for you."

"Oh! Thank you both so much."

They continued walking through a half empty house. Peter and Cindy had left behind a few things that they had kept of Hope's and Georgie's, and among those things, a picture that Hope had come across.

"Grandma, Georgie," she called. "Come here!"

"What's wrong, Hope?" asked Georgie.

"Look! Mom and Dad left us a great memory for us all, come see!"

It meant the world to Hope as Lynda and Georgie went to see what Hope was so excited about.

"What is it Hope?" asked her Grandma.

"Let me see," said Georgie.

Hope picked up a picture and showed them the picture of the family with a beautiful picture of Jesus in the background. It had inspired them so much.

"Don't you see," said Hope, "this means that Dad wanted us to know that we would never be alone or without the help of Jesus."

"You're right Hope," replied Georgie. "We will always be together and God will always be there for us wherever we are and whatever we do and no matter where we move. He will always show us the way. So, this picture was Dad's way of saying, God will be with all of us, as they travel to a new destination and we start some new beginnings."

Peter had already set up a room for his mother. He didn't want her to do a lot of moving, so when Lynda came to her room, she burst out into tears and couldn't believe that Peter had done this for her. She knew that he was the best son God could have ever blessed her with. She was so proud of him and thanked God for giving him to her and

George Sr.

There was one room left as Georgie walked around, he saw a sign on the wall. The sign read, "my son Georgie, you are the head of the household now. God has put you in here where there is faith and sunlight to light your world around you. The picture on the dresser will always remind you of how much we love you and the family. So, Georgie, thank you for taking over the boys school and watching over Grandma, all my love, Mom and Dad."

Georgie read it over and over, proud to know his father could trust him to care for the family while he was gone. God had given him a challenge that he wasn't sure he was ready for.

He took the letter to his Grandma and she read it and said, "Georgie your father has chosen you, as God has chosen him to do his work. You are a good boy and Hope and I are so happy you are here with us."

As they finished walking around, the three of them went outside and decided to go by Lynda's to get stuff packed to put in their new home, or still called Peter's home.

A week later, they drove to Alabama with Hope and enjoyed the scenery along the way, stopping here and there to rest and eat, reaching Hope's place early in the morning as they were glad to get there to rest up. They knew it would be another long ride home, so Georgie helped Hope get her stuff in the car, and packed a lunch for the way home. Hope only had her books and personal things because the apartment was furnished. So, it was easy for them not to have a heavy load. They spent the night by Hope's so they could get some good rest and good food. They toured some of the places around Alabama and called Peter in the morning to see how they were, and then headed home to Rome, Georgia.

"Well Hope, are you sure this is what you want to do?" Georgie asked. "It's a big step but a good one."

"Yes," she said, "God has shown me the way I should go. So yes, this is my decision. We will all three be fine, won't we Grandma?"

"Oh yes dear," Lynda replied, "and we will have lots of good times together. Lynda was thinking of her husband and how happy it would make him to know that there was someone with her. If only he was there with them to enjoy his grandchildren.

"Grandma," asked Georgie, "would you like to stop at the cemetery on the way home? We can all go and see Grandpa and Grandma Mary. I can tell that you were thinking about them."

"I would like that very much dear, if it's not too dark when we arrive there."

"We can check the flowers also," she said.

"Hope, are you okay?" As Georgie looked back and saw that Hope had fallen asleep. As he saw that she was sleeping, he didn't disturb her and continued to drive home.

"Grams," he said, "do you suppose we should stop so Hope can get something to eat? I worry about her."

"Well," Lynda said, "when she wakes up, we will stop for gas and eat something. I'm sure she will be fine Georgie," said Grandma.

Georgie drove a few more miles then stopped for gas and the three of them went in the restaurant area to eat and freshen up. George looked at Hope and Grandma asked, "would you two like to rest overnight or go on. It's been a long drive and maybe we could see some sites and start out early in the morning from Atlanta."

"Well," said Hope, "it's getting later and I would be good to walk around after we eat and see some stores and sites."

"How about you Grams?" she asked. Hope still had to keep her schedule.

"We can stay overnight and if you two want to walk to go see sites, it's okay, but I think I will just get settled in and relax if that's okay. It's been a long ride and I am very tired so you two go and enjoy yourselves," replied Lynda.

After eating, Georgie and Hope helped take the suitcases to their rooms and Lynda sat in her chair and was glad to be alone for awhile. Hope and her brother went walking and saw amazing things in the store windows. Hope saw some very pretty dresses that she would like but couldn't afford them.

"Oh, Georgie! Wouldn't that look great on Grandma? She would look ravishing in it."

"She sure would," Georgie replied.

"Should we go in and see it?"

They went in to the store and walked around, then stopped one of the clerks to ask, "Miss, how much is this dress?"

Hope had picked it up and carried it to the clerk. "Is it for you Miss?" the clerk asked.

"Oh no," said Georgi, "it's for our Grandma, she is at the hotel and we wanted to surprise her.

My sister and I thought she would look nice in it."

"Well," said the clerk, "I think that's wonderful idea."

The clerk looked at the price tag, and said (which was quite expensive), "this is the wrong price on here" and gave them a very good price that surprised the two of them.

"Wow," said Hope, "Grandma will love it Georgie."

"You bet she will and she deserves it," he said.

The two looked at each other and then looked at the clerk and said, "we will take it."

Hope was so happy, her face lit up like a sunbeam. "I am so glad the two of you like it, and I know your Grandma will too." "I wish I had grandchildren," said the clerk. They thanked her and told her that God loves her, and walked down the street proud that they had both agreed on Grandma's dress, and that God had sent an angel or they couldn't have gotten it.

They had gone back to the hotel and were tired and ready to call it a day. Hope slept with Lynda, and Georgie slept in a separate room The following morning, they prepared for a day's drive and asked God to be with them all the way, as he always is. Lynda had called Peter and Cindy to let them know that everything was fine, and that the twins had gone shopping and checked out the parks in the area. She didn't know about the gift they had gotten her but this was to be a surprise for her retirement party at the Christian school. Georgie and Hope would take over the school along with Jerry and John who have done wonderful work with the boys. Hope was going to call her Mom and Dad and see when they could make it home for a few days. It was to be a secret and surprise for Lynda.

As they arrived home that evening, they unloaded the car and Lynda said, "It is so good to be home."

Like Peter always said, there's no place like home and he was right. The house that the twins were born in was in their home, and they were proud to be back. It was late in the evening and it had been a long trip, but for Hope who had left her teaching job and her music, it was a difficult decision to make, but it made her feel good that she had come home. The three of them retired for the night and thanked God for safety and family.

The next morning, Lynda was up bright and early. She fixed the twins breakfast. As they were having breakfast together, they talked about what they would do that day as they each had their own ways to go.

"What are you going to do today, Hope?" asked Grandma.

Hope thought for a Moment and replied, "I guess I will just try to get things put away here first, and then join you and Georgie at the school, it that's alright."

"Of course it is," they answered.

"We are more than glad to have you come and join us as we want you to feel that you are doing what you want. You can introduce yourself to all the boys this afternoon, and you and Grandma can visit with them while I coach the boys at high school."

"That's a great idea," Hope said. "I can feel the boys out to see if there are enough of them for a boys choir, what do you think Grams?"

"That would be fine," said Lynda.

"I will see you both this afternoon at two p.m.," said Hope.

So excited she couldn't wait, if she could get the boys to sing, she would be very happy and she could be with her Grandma. Hope was excited about going to the boys school. She had been there with Grandpa Geroge when she was a little girl, and she followed him all around. She never gave it a thought that someday she would be doing some of grandpa's traditions.

"Can I do what God planned out for me?" she asked herself.

She continued to put things away in her room so she could meet Georgie and her Grandma at the school. When she finished she went to join them and they showed her that the boys were all gathered, and asked them to please sit down.

"Why?" asked Scott, who had just lost his mother.

"Scott," said Georgie, "we want you all to meet someone very special we think you all will like her."

"Who is it?" asked Scott.

"Well," Geroge said, "it is my twin sister Hope and she came to join us at the school, so welcome her here, okay?"

"Wow!" One of the boys yelled out, "I have a twin!"

"That's great," replied Georgie. "What is her name?"

The boys name is Alex. "My sister's name was Ellen, but she died when she was born."

"I am sorry to hear that," said Georgie. "Well, here is my sister, Hope, and let's give her a big hand to welcome her."

The boys stood and clapped their hands and said, "Welcome Miss Watkins."

"You can call me Hope if you like, and thank you for the welcoming. I will do the best I can to help each one of you. There is one thing that we are going to ask you all and that is, how do you feel about starting a boys choir?"

The boys all looked at one another and several of them spoke out excitedly, "Ya! That would be nice."

Hope and the staff smiled. "Great, we are hoping some of you would like that because Hope is going to be your teacher," said Georgie.

They continued their walk with Hope and she met a lot of nice people and was happy about starting her work on Monday. The family was settled down in their home that once was Peter and Cindy's. They missed their Mom and Dad, but had made a promise to take care of Grandma for them. Lynda was getting older and she tired out easily, so she didn't go to the boys school as often as she did when George Sr. and Peter were there. Hope and Georgie ran the school now, and John and Jerry were their staff members. Lynda would often work at the church so she could keep busy and keep her mind off Peter and Cindy. She often wished they were there, back home with the family. Hope and Georgie spent as much time with her at night as they could. Now that Hope was home, she had someone to talk to and enjoyed it very much. Because Georgie had a coaching job at night, and sometimes he would meet a young lady after games and take in a movie and stop to eat. He hadn't said anything to the family because it was only friends for awhile, but now it was getting more serious, they were becoming more than friends.

"The next time Georgie has a game," Hope asked her Grandma, "Grams, would you like to go and see one of Georgies games that he coaches tonight?"

Lynda was surprised because she had never watched her grandson coach.

They stayed until the end of the game, and waited for Georgie to surprise him and let him know that he was a great basketball coach. As Georgie walked over to the girl he had been going with, Hope yelled out, "George!"

George turned with a surprised look on his face, never expecting his sister and grandmother at the game.

"George, come over here for a minute," Hope said.

Georgie walked over by his grandmother and sister with the young lady that was with him.

"Grandma, what are you doing here?" he asked.

"Well, Hope and I decided it was time to see you in action Georgie, and you did a great job!"

"Yeah," said Hope, "we'll have to come more often, and gram's really enjoyed it."

As Georgie stood there with his girl, he put his arm around her and said, "Grams, Hope, this is Jenny Olsen."

"We were just going to stop and have a bite to eat, would you like to come with us?" Jenny asked.

George looked at her and replied, "Ya! We can all go together."

"Well, if we aren't in your way Georgie."

"No!" Jenny and George said. "You're never in the way Grams, come on Hope."

"Okay," she said and they joined together at a small restaurant, and Jenny joined right in with all three of them.

Then Hope and Lynda said, "Thanks for

inviting us, it was a pleasure to meet you Jenny."

"Thank you George, and we will see you at home. It was very nice meeting you Jenny," as they left they waved goodbye and returned to the car.

"Grandma," said Hope, "how long has George known this girl? She seems like a very friendly person."

"I don't know dear," said Lynda, "I didn't know he was dating anyone but yes, she does seem to be very nice and good for him."

They reached home and they were ready for the evening bible readings, but it seemed different, "Something isn't right," said Lynda.

"Why Grandma?" asked Hope, wondering if Grandma was okay, "what's wrong?"

"Well, Peter and Cindy are gone away, and now Georgie isn't home for the bible reading and I really miss your grandpa, he always made me laugh and before long Georgie will want to be on his own, maybe even married!"

"Well, I'm here Grandma and I don't think Georgie will be far away," Hope said, "so don't worry! Even if he does get married, he will always be here for us, and remember Mom and Dad aren't going to be gone forever! They will be home before you know it."

"Okay dear, we will wait a few minutes for George to do our readings."

They grabbed a glass of milk and sat quietly when they heard Georgie arrive.

"Is that you Georgie?" asked Lynda.

"Yes Grams, I will be right there, I'm glad you waited up we can all do our reading together. I'm sorry I'm late Grams," he said.

"That's alright, come into the sitting room so we can read."

As the three sat and read, it was quiet. George lead the prayer for the night and it seemed like Peter and Cindy were right there with them and it was a good feeling. They were able to rest for the night as each one looked at the pictures and memories that Peter had left in the house for God's comfort. They were signs that God would always be there for them.

The following week was a hard one for Hope, and yet a happy one. She started work at the Christian school and the boys accepted her with open hearts. There were several boys about twelve who began to sing in the boys choir to start with, but as the week passed, several more had joined in. She began to enjoy her work because that's what she loved doing. The boys were very enthusiastic about singing.

One day, Hope had heard one of the boys playing the piano when she came in to work one afternoon. She was so amazed. She stood and listened in silence to the boy who was also named Peter. She sat down beside him and said, "Peter you play very well, where did you learn to play?"

"Well, ma'am, my mother taught me when I was six years old, and she made me play every day for one hour."

Peter started getting tears in his eyes, but didn't want Hope to notice but she did.

"Peter, what is it?" she asked.

"Well, my mother died a year ago, so I play piano to remember her by."

Hope was speechless for a few minutes, until she said, "Peter, your Mom and Dad should be very proud of you. You know what, my Dad's name is Peter also. He is a minister and maybe you can play at our church on Sunday, how would you like that?"

"I don't know Hope. I never played for anyone before," replied Peter. "You really think it will be okay?"

"Sure it will," said Hope.

She had found a young boy who had the

same dream she had when she was younger. She gathered the boys for practice and even asked Peter Manning to play a solo. The boys clapped their hands as they had never heard Peter play piano before. It made Peter feel really good. The choir started like a really good Choir. Georgie came in, just as they were singing their last song, which was, "Jesus Loves Me."

"Wow!" He said, "that sounded great, that was a beautiful sound, you could even sing that at church."

"Hope! Grandma and I will talk to the church, okay?"

"That's wonderful Georgie. It would be our first time singing in public."

Hope was so ecstatic that her brother enjoyed the boys choir.

"Hope, you did a beautiful job. I know the church will love the choir and the boys will do great."

The weeks passed and Lynda and George were so proud of them that they began to sing every other Sunday at the church. Hope knew that God had given her so much and let her do the one thing she loves the most, that she even let Peter Manning play piano for the boys. Peter could play anything you put in front of him. The congregation loved the choir and asked Hope to lead the adult choir, rather than the children's choir at church.

Hope met with the staff at church and said, "Most of you know me from my childhood in Sunday school, and I am grateful that you have asked me to lead the children's choir but I do not want to take anyone's job away from them."

"But, Hope!" said one of the board members, "we don't have a choir director, that's why we are all here to ask you to do it."

"We have seen the beautiful work you have done at the boys school, and that's why we would like to have you join us on staff here," replied Jon Hensen chairman.

"Well, Hope," said Georgie, "will you do this for the church? They really need a good Choir director."

"I can't believe it," she said, "I come home looking for work and God sends me two blessings. I..I will be glad to accept the job."

Tears rolled down her face and Georgie walked over to her and embraced her and said to her, "I am very proud of my twin sister."

She turned to the staff and said, "how can I

thank you?"

"Well, by starting next week at your time and day," said Mr. Hansen.

"Welcome to our staff Hope, we are glad to have you back."

"Thanks," Hope said, "I will do my best."

Hope and Georgie left for home to tell Lynda, who was busy preparing dinner.

"Grams," called the twins, "where are you?"

"I'm in the kitchen kids, what's wrong?" Grandma said.

Hope all excited and happy said, "I..I got a job at the church - I'm going to teach the children's choir at church, isn't it great," as she put her arms around Grandma Watkins.

"I can't wait to call Dad and Mom."

"Oh, Hope," her Grandma said, "that's wonderful."

"Well, come and we'll all have our dinner and thank God for all he has given us."

As they continued their dinner and the dishes were done, Georgie told them he was going to see Jenny if they didn't need anything done. Lynda agreed, everything was okay and told Georgie he could go, but she would like him to bring Jenny over for church.

"I will be glad to Grams, I think that's a good idea since you both met her the other night," George replied.

Hope was so excited and couldn't wait to call her Dad and Mom. After she called them, she and Grandma Lynda sat down to the piano and sang a couple of Christian songs together.

Then Lynda asked Hope, what day's she would have at church and what day's at the school. "I don't know yet Grams. I have to set it up with the boys at school, and then I will know. Peter, one of the boys can play piano at school. Does he go to church Grandma?"

"Just at the school chapel," she said. "He is one of our newer boys, but a very good person, like most of the boys his Dad travels a lot on the job, and his Mom puts in many hours at the hospital. They are good parents and teaches Peter right from wrong," replied Lynda.

Hope enjoyed working with the boys at school and scheduled her time with her young children at church. The church was proud of her work. She became a very busy lady, sometimes she would have the boys choir join the church choir, and it was beautiful.

One weekend, Peter and Cindy surprised them, his Mom was in the kitchen getting breakfast together when she heard a knock on the door and called "Georgie, please get the door."

Peter didn't want to walk in, he wanted to see his mothers face when he and Cindy walked in. Georgie went to the door, and much to his surprise looked at his Dad and Mom, and called, "Grandma! Grandma, Hope? Come here, hurry!"

As he gave them a hug, "we are coming George," they called as they went out to see who had come so early in the morning. As they got to the door, Hope said, "Mom, Dad, we are so happy so see you, why didn't you call?"

She gave them a hug and said Grams, "look at who is here."

Lynda, so surprised said, "Peter, Cindy, how good to see you! Come on in, we have missed you so much," and the tears rolled down her cheeks.

"Now the family is all together, did you have breakfast," she asked?

"No Mom," said Peter and Cindy.

"Well, come on, we're just sitting down now."

And they all sat together and Georgie gave

the blessings.

"Dad," George said, "how long are you staying?"

"Well," replied Peter, "we will fly back Sunday evening, but we missed our family and had to come and hear Hope's choir sing on Sunday. We heard you were doing so well Hope.

"I love it Dad, it is so much fun working with young children, it's a gift sent from heaven, they are all very good singers, you will love them Mom."

They visited all hours of the night until they began to get tired and gathered together and prayed. In the morning, they rose early and Cindy and Peter took the family out to breakfast. Lynda, Peter's Mom, wanted to fix it for them but Peter refused to have her cooking over a hot stove. After breakfast out, they drove to the church, and Peter sat with his family as the other pastor form the boys home read the opening prayer and song. Then he looked up and to his surprise, he was quiet and saw Peter.

He said to the congregation, "we have a special visitor here today that many of you know. Peter would you come up and greet the people? We were so surprised to see you, what are you doing here," he asked?

"Well, Cindy and I missed all of you but we came to see how well our daughter Hope is doing with the choir."

"Oh, she is great with the children," replied Pastor Olson. "We are blessed to have her, would you read the scriptures Peter?"

Peter read the bible readings and introduced himself to those he didn't know after church. Peter greeted each one as they left the services. Many familiar faces were glad to see him and Cindy. Some even asked when they were coming home.

"Well," said Peter, "the church in Louisiana is doing better, but it will be another couple years before we may return, we want to be sure that whoever is chosen to take over, is what the church needs to keep them going and believing in Jesus Christ. They have some heavy problems, but I think they are on the way to recovery, so we can all pray that God watches over all of them, Right?"

"You bet," said a few members who were listening to Peter.

"Well, I must say goodbye to all for now, and hope to see you soon."

"God bless you all," as they left, they waved goodbye and went to say goodbye to Jerry and John and thanked them for talking over the weekend.

It was all too soon, and Peter and Cindy were at the airport with the family saying goodbye and shedding tears as they boarded the plane. Leaving Hope and Georgie was hard, but leaving his mother was harder.

"We love you all," they called from the gate.

Hope replied back, "We love you Daddy."

They were all three quiet as they drove home.

Then Hope spoke and said, "Wasn't it wonderful to see Dad and Mom?"

"It sure was," replied Lynda and George.

Then they started singing songs of joy and happiness together. After Georgie had gotten everyone home, he called Jenny and wished she had been with them. Lynda was very tired and went to her room to rest for awhile. Hope went to play her piano and was humming along. Lynda loved listening to her granddaughter sing. She had such a beautiful voice. George had paperwork to do, so he went to the office to catch up on it, wishing Jenny was there beside him.

The following week was a normal work week. They all went on to do what God had for them to do. George hadn't seen Jenny since the weekend. Jenny was a teacher, and George was busy at the boys school, and when it came to Saturday, George had a little league ball game, so Jenny surprised him and went to watch him coach the team. At half time, he looked up and saw Jenny standing there and joined her for a soda, "What are you doing here?"

She smiled at him and said, "I missed you and remembered you had a game and had to surprise you."

"You sure did, but what a nice surprise," Georgie replied and hugged her gently.

"Wait for me until after the game okay?"

"Yes, I'll be right here," Jenny said.

After the game, Georgie and Jenny went home and went riding around and decided to take in a movie. After the movie he took Jenny home and he went home to see how things were. His Grandma and Hope were waiting for George, wondering where he had gone after his game with the boys.

When George arrived, "George? Where have you been? We have been worried about you," his Grandma replied.

"Oh, I am sorry Grams, I should have called. I met Jenny at the ball game and afterwards we went to a movie."

George was a grown man now and didn't think he needed to explain what he does with his time, but he was glad that his sis and Grams was worried about him.

"Grams, I'm happy that you worry about me, but you know I am grown up now, so please… don't wait up for me okay? I will try to remember to call if Jenny and I are going to be late, okay? I love you gram very much."

The morning was a beautiful bright one, and the three of them had breakfast together and went their separate ways to work. Before they left, George had asked Hope if she was coming over to the boys school today. He thought it would be neat to hear the boys and her sing.

"Oh, sure, why George?" she asked.

"Well, the boys love starting their days with a song in their heart."

"I certainly will be there George, it will be after they are done with breakfast and making their beds, how does that sound?" Hope asked.

"That will be great," he replied.

As they parted different directions for the day, "See you later sis."

Hope had said goodbye to her Grandma, and asked her if she would like to go to school with her when she gets back from the church. She had some paperwork to do first and some parents to talk to, then she would come and get her.

"I would love to go hear the boys sing, oh I wish Peter could be here and Cindy. They would be so proud of you and George."

She turned her head so Hope didn't see tears running down her cheek, but Hope could hear it in her voice as she gave her Grandma a hug, and said she would be back soon. Hope felt bad that she had to leave Lynda, also knowing how sad she was, but she said, "I must get to the church, or they will wonder if I'm coming or not."

She left to go, but looked back and waved to her Grandma and said, "I will be back to get you, okay?"

Lynda smiled and waved goodbye, and went in to keep herself busy, still wishing Peter and Cindy were there with her.

After a year, George and Hope missed their Dad and Mom, and were wondering how long it would be before they return home for good. They had been gone now for four years and Grandma was getting tired, and couldn't get around like she had been, but she knew George would need more help at the school as he couldn't do it alone.

George and Hope sensed there was something wrong with their Grandma and thought it would be best to call Peter and Cindy. They wondered if Grandma was sick or if something was seriously wrong. When night time came, they all gathered around the fireplace. Lynda picked up the bible and read from it.

She said to the twins, "I remember when your grandpa found Peter lying on the street downtown unconscious, not knowing who or where he came from."

"But Grams, did you and grandpa adopt Peter? How old was he?"

The twins were flabbergasted because they didn't know that their Dad was adopted by their Grandma and grandpa. She continued to tell them the story of Peter, and how much he means to her and George Sr. She became tired and the twins asked her if she would like to talk to Peter. Her eyes sparkled at the question. Georgie made a phone call to his Dad and surprised his Grandma.

"Oh George, that, that would be very nice to hear his voice."

"Well, Grams, here, take the phone and say hello."

Lynda answered the phone not knowing Peter was on it.

"Hello?" she said, and the voice on the other end answered.

"Mom.. Is..Is that you? This is Peter."

"Yes Peter, it's me, what a surprise to hear your voice again, I miss you, how are you?" She continued, being so excited she started weeping of joy, "when are you coming home?"

"The twins are so busy and Georgie has a girlfriend, it sounds serious."

She talked quite a while to Peter and then said, "I love you, Peter, come home soon, okay?"

And she handed the phone to Hope, and she gave them both a hug and said goodnight. Hope took the phone first and then Georgie took the phone and explained how much Lynda needed them, and that he thought there was something going on with her.

"I don't think she's feeling well Dad, but she doesn't tell us anything, she's tired a lot and doesn't eat much, she really worries us, Dad, when can you come home? We need you and Mom."

To Georgie's surprise, Peter answered Georgies question with an answer George didn't expect.

"Well, soon, when Dad?"

"We'll, keep it a secret because Mom and I are moving back the first of the month, in two weeks George but please, keep it a secret okay?"

"Okay Dad, that's wonderful. Do you have a place to say Dad? Yes, Georgie, we checked into some houses when we were there."

"Oh Dad! I am so glad to hear that. Is there anything that Hope and I can do? If there is, give me a call… at work. Dad, Grams will be so happy. Hope and I will take good care of her, you and Mom take care, we will be waiting for your home coming, love ya Dad, please tell Mom that we love her to, bye bye."

Peter's Return

Keeping Peter's secret from Lynda and Hope was a difficult for Georgie because he was worried about his Grandma. How could he do it? He was so excited, and wanted to tell her but he couldn't. Lynda was getting up in age now but wouldn't give up going to the boy's school and helped where she could. She felt closer to George, her husband, there. That was his dream to help any boy that was in trouble. John and Jerry are the ones that came back, and now help George Jr. as if they belong. The boys, John and Jerry, were always willing to because he had helped them get through hard times as young boys. George thought just … just maybe they could help them give a welcome home party at the school, and Hope could play some songs. But how was he going to ask her without spilling the beans? The boys would have to ask her to do some on that day. They only had two weeks, so he had to get things going with John and Jerry, and Pastor Olson who was glad to hear that Peter was coming home. As things were going good in Shreveport, Peter asked to be home to spend time with his family. He knew his mother was getting older and they had gotten a reliable pastor to take his place. Peter was sure he would be liked by the members, and help the church do things together and grow. It has gotten many new members since Pastor Rogers had come to join them. Pastor Rogers worked alongside Peter and was amazed to see how wonderful the members had accepted him as their new Pastor. Pastor Rogers joined in with church activities, and had many invitations to join friends and members at their home. If he wasn't sure Pastor Rogers would be a blessing to Shreveport Christian Church, he would never ask to leave.

A week passed and Peter and Cindy were busy packing and letting the members know how wonderful it was to be their Pastor for the last five years.

"I have met so many wonderful people, and will miss all of them," he said to Pastor Rogers.

"But now I leave it in God's hands and I know you will do wonders."

When it got closer to the last week, Peter and Cindy planned a church picnic so they could say goodbye and inform everyone that Pastor Rogers would be their minister.

"Cindy and I will always remember the experience that God has given us to serve you all. We are very proud to be part of your growing church and to know all of you. I will miss all of you here, but the time comes when one must return to where God sends us. So, Cindy and I will say goodbye to all of you and know that you are in good hands with Pastor Rogers. Pastor Rogers is married to a wonderful lady and has two grown children, as do I. There is nothing you can't talk to him about if you need to, okay? Now, before Cindy and I go home, we would like to thank you for your kindness and your support to bring your church out of trouble and help it grow in God's grace. So, let's ask Pastor Rogers to say a prayer for closing our day."

As he said the prayer, they all wished Peter and Cindy God's love and blessings and handed them a beautiful farewell plaque which said, "God Bless you for bringing our Church back to life again," signed by the staff and members of the Shreveport Christian Church. How proud Peter was as he thanked them all with tears streaming down his cheeks. They all clapped their hands and Peter said goodbye to all, and hoped that someday they would be back to visit. Sad, but excited to be moving home, he wanted to be close to his mother who had given him so much to live for since he was a little boy. Now it was his turn to give back some of the love that she and his father had given him. Now it was his turn to take care of his mother and care for her before he lost her.

When they got home that night from the church picnic, Cindy asked Peter, "do you think your Mom will be surprised?"

"I sure hope so," replied Peter. "Georgie is very good at keeping things quiet. Now that he has a girl, she will help him get things organized along with Jerry and John. George said that they are having a problem at school and wanted us to be there."

"That sounds great," Cindy said, "I will love that."

As they looked around the parsonage, they thought of all the good times they had and all the new friends they were going to miss. They prayed together that God would keep the church growing and that God would continue to guide Pastor Rogers.

Time was going so fast, and Peter and Cindy were almost done packing and waiting for the truck to arrive. Meanwhile, he gave his son George a call to see how things were back home.

"Dad, we are doing fine and Grandma is okay. She will be so happy to see you both, and Hope and I will. Hope doesn't yet know, she is giving a concert at the school the day after you arrive, so she will really...be surprised! How is Mom? Tell her I love her and we will see you Sunday night. Dad, we love you."

The day had come when Peter and Cindy were ready to head home to Rome, Georgia, the little town he had grown up in and raised his children. As they went to get in the car, many of the neighbors had come over to say goodbye and wish them a safe trip home. How pleased Peter and Cindy were to see them off.

"We will miss you all," he said and, "may the glory of God bless you all." As they drove away, they waved goodbye, as did all the neighbors until they were out of sight. Traveling home was a two day drive, they would stop at a hotel, they thought how quiet and peaceful it was. Their room had a large window where they could look out and see the beautiful sunset, and it reminded Peter of the one he was in when he was in college and where he had met Cindy and how frail she was.

He asked, "remember the times we had when we first met?"

"Sure I do Peter."

"Well, remember when we looked out the window like this, and the sun was a beautiful sunset like this one, do you remember what I said?"

"Yes, Peter, I certainly do, How could I ever forget? You looked at me with a glow in your eyes like ... now," and she turned to him and said, "you... you asked me to marry you and I said yes."

Peter looked at her, bent down and kissed her. "It was the best day of my life, and you and your Mom have always been there for me, as my Dad and Mom are."

They talked for a while, bringing back old memories of the past and how God has gotten them through hard times in Shreveport but were glad to be going home to their family and friends. In the morning, as they arose and were ready to stop and have breakfast, they had called George and told him that they would see him at the school around 4 p.m.. He figured that would be about the earliest they could make it. George was glad to hear that Peter and Cindy were okay and that they would be home soon, but he didn't know how to tell that they couldn't meet there.

"Why?" asked Peter.

"Well, Dad, they have a big meeting there tonight so maybe we can meet at the church, is that alright?"

"Sure, George, that will be fine."

"Okay then, we will see you and Mom tomorrow."

As they were driving home, Peter saw a young boy sitting on the curb of the road, "doesn't he look sad and lost Cindy?"

"He sure does," she replied.

"He looks like he's lost with nowhere to go. Do you think we should go back and get him?"

"He looked pretty hungry - maybe we better before he wanders into the road."

"I was hoping you would say that dear."

As they drove down to the next turn off, they turned around and saw that they young boy was still sitting there. It was a hot day and the boy was getting burned from the sun. As Peter turned into a driveway, he and Cindy got out and walked over to the boy.

"Are you lost young man?" came a voice he didn't recognize and stood up slowly as he was very weak.

"Who are you?" asked the young boy.

The boy was short and wearing torn clothes. He looked up at Peter and said, "my name is Mike, who are you and what do you want?"

"My name is Peter, and this is my wife Cindy, we saw you sitting here when we went past and thought that you might need a friend, so we turned around to see if we could help. Where do you live, Mike?"

As he sat down by Mike, he noticed how thin the young boy was. Mike looked are Peter and slowly answered "I.. stayed at my foster home but I didn't like it there, they were too mean and they wouldn't let me do anything. They didn't like me, so I ran away. I don't want to go back. Please... please...don't take me back there," the boy cried out.

"I will just run away again, so just go away."

As tears ran down his cheeks and he started to walk away from the one who wanted to help him, Peter pulled him back and caressed the boy against him.

"It's alright son, we will find out what to do, but we must call the authorities to see what we can do. Can you show us where the police department is?" asked Peter. "We can't leave you in this hot sun."

"No! NO! You will make me go back to the bad people."

"No…no we won't Mike," said Cindy. "We will help you through this day, okay?"

"Okay," said Mike, as they went to the car. Mike became quiet as he sat in the backseat. Cindy had checked on him and saw that he was sound asleep.

"He was so exhausted. That poor boy," she said he must have had a hard life and she happened to think of meeting George at 4, but it was already getting late. "Peter! We need to call George and let him know we will be late! He will get worried."

"Oh, yes dear, as soon as we find the police station."

"Cindy," Peter said, "please stay in the car until I talk to the officer, okay? I won't be long. If Mike wakes up please bring him in."

"But Peter, what if he doesn't come with me, he might take off again, please take him with you."

Peter woke up Mike so as to not have anything happen to him. Mike was a 14-year-old boy with dark hair and blue eyes, and about 4 feet tall. Cindy was worried she wouldn't be able to talk him into going in with her, so she was relieved when Peter decided to take him in with them. Mike didn't give them any trouble. Peter asked Mike where his parents were and if he could call them, but Mike was quiet and replied, "I don't know where they are and I don't care. They don't care about me or they wouldn't have left me."

"Okay, we'll find out and if we can't, we will get permission to take you home with us if that 's okay with you Mike."

Mike didn't know what to say, he thought "gee these seem like very nice people, why are they doing this for me?"

Finally he asked, "then, why...why would you want to take me home with you?"

"Well, Mike, I am a minister and you are one of God's children."

"What do you mean? I don't know who God is."

"Haven't you ever gone to Sunday school?"

"Why," Mike asked?

"Well, they learn about God and Jesus and

helping other people like you, who are lost and feel they have no place in life," Peter told him.

"And our daughter teaches music and the choir," Cindy added. "So, we think you will like it there. Peter also runs a Christian Boy's school. There are many boys in your situation. So, you decided Mike what you want to do, alright?"

As they walked into the police station, in a little town called Shiloh, they all three were silent and were still 100 miles from home, and knew George would be waiting and wondering why they were going to be late. As they reached the police station door, Mike stopped and didn't want to go in.

"They will send me back Mr. Watkins, I don't want to!"

"We will talk to them, okay? But you have to tell them what happened to you, can you do that for us Mike?"

"I guess so," he said very softly. When they entered the station, an officer came up to them and introduced himself as Officer John Smith.

"What can I do for you folks?" he asked in a harsh voice.

"Well," said Peter, "we have a young lad that we picked up on our way home to Rome, GA.

We are moving back home where the rest of our family is waiting for us."

"How may I help you?" asked the officer. "Where did you pick him up, and why was he there?"

"I'm sorry sir, I didn't get your name?"

Peter introduced himself and Cindy to the officer, and began to tell him where he picked Mike up. "Well, he was about 2 miles down the road sitting on the side of the road by himself, so we turned around and took him with us. But we don't know where his parents are."

"Where are your parents?" the officer asked.

Mike started to walk away, and Peter said, "Mike we have to tell the officer or we cannot help you, alright?"

Mike went over by Officer Smith and answered, "I don't know. They put me in a foster home and they were to mean, we and the other 2 kids never had much to eat or could do anything, so I wanted to leave there and I did. I don't want to go back there. Please. Don't make me."

"Do you have their names so we can call the social worker? We need to know so we can tell them you are alright; they may come down here to talk to you."

"Well, I, I'm, not going there; I can take care of myself."

"Mike, you, you don't have to be alone. If the social worker approves it, and you would like to, you can come home with us. It will be nice to have a young child in the house again. Won't it, Cindy?"

"Our twins, you have twins?" Mike asked in a very surprised voice.

"Yes, but they are grown up now, and as busy as they can be, so what do you think Mike?"

"That sounds very nice Peter, but will the police let me?"

"I don't know Mike. They may want to find your mother and father first. If they do, we will have to respect their wishes and I know God will find a way for you."

As they continued talking to Officer Smith, Peter asked what they should do.

"Well," said the officer, "I can't let him go with you until we get permission from one of the other parents because he is aware of the court."

"I'm sorry Mike, Cindy and I will have to leave you and will get in touch with you tomorrow, my son is waiting for us and we must go okay? They will get worried if we don't show up."

"No, no don't leave me - you said you would

take me with you!"

"I can't Mike, because I need a consent form from your parents. I would be doing something wrong but, if it's okay with them, we will come back and get you as soon as they let us know okay?"

"Alright, but you will come back won't you?"

"You bet we will, Mike!" Peter gave him a hug and embraced him, but he didn't want to leave him, a young desperate boy who wanted someone to love him.

Peter left Mike with the officer, and left his address and phone number where he could reach him, also leaving the number of the boy's school. The officer took Mike after they said goodbye in his office and let Mike see what policemen do. Mike was enjoying talking and meeting with other officers. Cindy and Peter went to the car but were worried about the boy and what would happen to him. As Peter started driving, Cindy took his hand and they prayed that Mike would find his parents and be happy. As they got closer to home, Peter called George to let him know what time they could be there, they were going to stop for something to eat first, and then they would be on their way home. They were to meet him at the church so Cindy and he wouldn't know what was going on the next day at the school. The boy's that knew the Watkins were anxious to see them.

As Peter and Cindy drove into town, they stopped at the cemetery first, and then to the church. He couldn't go home because it was a surprise for Hope and Lynda who had no idea they were coming home to stay. But Peter's mind wandered back to Mike and was curious to know how he was.

"I will call them tomorrow," he thought to himself as he turned into the church parking lot. George was waiting at the door to meet them with open arms.

"George! How are you? Have you been waiting long?" they asked him.

"Well, yes. But we had a church meeting first so that time went a little faster, but we're sure glad to have you back home Mom!"

Some of Peter's church members, who knew him, welcomed them home and were glad to see them. George and his parents talked for quite a while, they told George about Mike and what a sad situation it was.

"Dad, why didn't you bring him with you, we could have helped the lad?"

"We couldn't George, because he was a ward of the state. They had to find one of his parents to get permission, but we do plan to go see him soon."

"Georgie, let's go home and see how things are at the new house," Cindy suggested.

"Sure, Mom, are you ready Dad?"

"I sure am Son!"

They locked up the church and headed for Peter and Cindy's home. George had never seen it so it was a surprise for him. He gazed at the sight of it, not a big house, but a very beautiful place. He loved it. It was a nice size for his Mom to keep up with, and maybe Grandma Watkins would move in with them as she was getting older and it was hard for her to get around even though she didn't want to be treated like an invalid. After showing the house, Peter and Cindy thanked George for keeping their secret and told him they would see him and Mom at the school in the morning.

"Make sure your Grandma is there," and he smiled and said, "see you tomorrow."

George said, "Goodnight Mom and Dad, see you at 11:00 tomorrow."

As the evening passed, George called Jenny

and talked for hours. "Jenny can you come to the concert at school tomorrow?" he asked her.

"Sure Peter, why?"

"There's someone I would like you to meet."

"Okay!" Jenny was excited and pleased that George had called and she would be glad to see him, they haven't seen much of each other lately because he had been so busy getting things ready for his Mom and Dad. After they were through talking, they closed by saying goodbye, and see you tomorrow. George checked on his Grandma in the next room sleeping and Hope was sound asleep.

"That's good," he said.

As the sun rose bright and very pretty, Lynda was up preparing the coffee and setting up the breakfast as she usually had. She had no idea what she was going to do, maybe she would go listen to Hope and the kids practice at church. She loves going there. She called Hope and George out to eat breakfast. As they said their morning prayer Hope and George added, "let Grandma have a happy day."

Hope knew she had to be at the school for the concert, but didn't know her Mom and Dad were home. She and her Grandma would be so surprised. And they went their own way. George had gone to school and helped the staff get ready for the homecoming of Peter. Jerry and John were so excited, they were regular staff members now, and would Peter remember them?

John said to Jerry, "it will be good to see Peter, won't it John?"

"It sure will, he is a wonderful person."

John remembered when he ran away and Peter found him at the bus station waiting to go see his grandmother, she was the one who cared about him. Peter found him lying on a park bench in the cold and took him for a ride and talked with him about God and how he helped him through all the bad times. He owed Peter a lot and wanted it to be a nice homecoming for him.

As eleven o'clock arrived, they all were waiting for Hope to start the music as Hope and her Grandma arrived at the door to see many of the boys waiting in the dining area.

"I will see you later Grams. I need to get the boys all set for their song okay?"

"I will wait with the boys so I can hear it," Lynda replied. Also asking, "what is the occasion, Hope?"

"Nothing Grams," Hope didn't know herself. To

her it was just a special concert to see how the boys were doing. She was very proud of them. As Hope gathered the boys together, Lynda visited with the other ones and then with Reverend Olson, she was excited to hear them sing.

"Well Mrs. Watkins, what do you think?" Pastor Olson asked.

"She has done wonders with them," Lynda said. "She plays the piano so well, I am very proud of her."

As she and pastor were talking, Georgie walked up to them and quieted everyone down.

"They are coming! So everyone yell welcome home, okay?"

As Cindy and Peter walked to the room, everyone called out "Welcome Home Mr. and Mrs. Watkins."

Some knew him as Peter, Peter was very surprised. "Georgie, why didn't you say something about this? It is so good to see all of you," he replied and then the boys and Hope marched in to sing several songs that they practiced. Cindy and Peter were amazed as they sat down in the front row with Pastor Olson and were proud of Hope and what she has done for the school. After singing in the concert which had a happy applause to it, Pastor Olson announced "we have something Scott wants to read to you all."

Scott went up to the front and started reading a poem he saw in a paper. The name of it is "Friends" he announced.

God made dear friends like you
Friends with love, pride and truth
Friends who sing and shout
Most of all, friends to care about
Friends to share a tear or two
A smile, a dream or something new
It takes a friend's smile, so cheerful and bright
Just to know our heavenly father is in sight

We see his face and know He's near
And still sometimes we feel great fear
Hand and hand, we walk with him
The one who forgave us our sins
And the one who brought us together as friends

After he finished he said, "this is a special poem for all of you because you helped me through a rough time when my Mom died.

It meant a lot to me and that you cared and shared your friendship with me, thank you very much."

Scott got a big applause and Hope and the boy's sang, "Seek Ye First the Kingdom of God" and all joined in. After the song, John and Jerry and the staff asked Peter to come up front, as he walked they up greeted him. "Very happy to have you home Peter, we would like to welcome you back home Peter, we would like to welcome you back home and would like you to have something from all of us here," said John.

Jerry turned to unveil the surprise they had made. "Peter we would like to present this plaque to you for all you have taught us and supporting us in rough times."

Peter smiled with tears running down his eye. "I … I am speechless," he said. "I thank you all, and you have all done a wonderful job while I was away." Cindy and Lynda were so proud of the boys.

Hope was surprised because Georgie had kept the secret from all of them. As they gathered around the table buffet style, Pastor Olson asked Peter to say grace and then they all joined in the eating and talking and greeting Peter and Cindy home. Lynda went over by Peter and Cindy, tears in her aging eyes, put her arms around them and said, "I am so happy you are home, why didn't you tell me?"

"We wanted it to be a special surprise for you, Mom, so what do you think of our boy's?" Peter asked. "Aren't they wonderful?"

"They sure are, Son. Georgie and Hope have done wonderful things with them."

"They sure have, we are very proud of them."

"George and Hope? There's plenty of room with us."

"I think it's time they had their own place Mom. They are old enough and besides, they have their friends to entertain. But Mom, you can come live with us, okay? We even have a special room for you, so if you want to lie down and rest you can."

"Well, thank you so much Son, you and Cindy are so thoughtful. Are you sure you don't want to be alone?"

"Mother," Peter said, "since we had you in mind when we bought the house, so say you will, okay?"

"I would love to kids, thank you so much. I love you both. Oh Peter, has Georgie told you anything about Jenny, she is a very sweet girl."

"Well, he introduced us at the surprise party. Is it serious Mom?"

"I'm not sure, but they see a lot of each other, you will have to have them over for dinner when you get settled in son, you will have Cindy."

"I'm sure we will, Mom."

As the party ended and everyone said goodnight, Peter and Cindy took Lynda home and then drove to their place. "It has been a long day dear hasn't it? But wonderful to see everyone again."

"It sure was," Peter answered. "John and Jerry have grown into very good men. They're not boys anymore. I would be proud to have them as part of our family."

"Say, Cindy," said Peter, "I think I better call the police department in Shiloh to see what happened to Mike, I hope he's okay. I'll call first thing in the morning to let him know we haven't forgotten the lad."

"Sounds like a good idea idea, but now we need to arrange our house so we know where things are. I'm so happy that Mom is here, she can sit and look out the window while she is sewing or reading."

"I know she will love it."

The evening went so fast, but the day was wonderful for Peter and Cindy, they read their scriptures and were ready to crawl into bed. Peter put his arms around Cindy, kissed her goodnight, and said "this is a day we will never forget dear."

"No," replied Cindy, "it's good to be back home and lying close to each other." And they fell asleep in peace. The next morning as they rose, they looked around the house to make sure everything was okay and the room they planned for Lynda was in the best conditions for her. The movers had delivered all their furniture so all they needed to do was to move Lynda's things over and talk to Georgie and Hope. They were grown up now.

Peter called Hope first and asked her if she and George would go out for dinner with them. "Sure Dad, that would be nice. I will ask George, oh…Dad, maybe… you better ask him, alright?"

"Okay dear, I'll stop at the school tomorrow, well you have a good night Hope and I love you."

The next morning, Peter called Shiloh's police department and was lucky to get the same officer that took Mike. "Hello," said Captain Smith, "how may I help you?"

"Captain Smith, this is Peter Watkins from

Georgia. I called to see what has happened to Mike, the young boy that we brought into you, how is he doing?"

"Well," said officer Smith, "we couldn't reach either of his parents, so he was sent to stay at the foster home."

"Well," said Peter, "that's too bad. I thought you would find one of them, is it alright if my wife and I come to see him? I promised Mike that we would be back to see him."

"I think that would be fine, sir," replied Captain Smith. "He is in a different home now, when you get here, we will give you his address."

"We thought a lot about Mike and wondered how he was doing. Cindy and I will be down next Saturday to visit him, if that's okay and the foster parents are okay with it," replied Peter.

"I will let the foster parents know," said Captain Smith, "and will call you back tomorrow."

"That will be fine, thank you sir," said Peter. As he hung up the phone, Cindy asked him, "how is he, where is he, can we see him?"

"Wait … Cindy one question at a time, please! Well, he said they didn't find his parents and he is at a new foster home. The police are going to check with Mike and the new parents if we can see him and if we can, he will call us sometime tomorrow."

"So, if we can when will we go?" asked Cindy all excited.

"I told the officer we would see him next weekend, is that alright dear?"

"Oh yes dear, that would be nice, I pray he is okay, he sure was unhappy. Do you think Mother would like to go?"

"I think that will be too long of a ride for her dear."

"I guess you're right Peter, she will be happy just to have her own room and can sit outside."

The following week was a busy one. Lynda had moved in with Cindy and Peter. George and Hope missed her very much, but stopped by to see her quite often during the week. George and Hope accepted the fact that they would be alone and needed to take responsibility now. They were gone so much during the day and nights with both of them working many hours. Jenny came over with George as often as she could, she helped fix meals, but one day George had come home from school. Like usual he would check the mail, he put all the bills together but there was one letter that didn't look familiar. As he picked it up and looked at it and the words read U.S. Army Government. He opened it, afraid of what is meant, he was shocked!

"Oh, no," he said, "they can't do this!" As he was very upset, he called his Dad. "Dad...Dad...I got a letter from the U.S. Army. Can you no... wait...I'll bring it over there," it was only a few blocks away.

Hope was still at church with the choir. As George arrived at his Dad's house, Peter and Cindy and Grandma were waiting at the door. "Mom, Dad.... Do I have to go? There must be some mistake."

Peter took the letter and read it over. "I am so sorry son, you are called for duty, there is no getting out of it son."

"Oh, Peter, and Cindy, why Georgie? He can't go, we need him here, what is Hope going to do by herself?" Tears came to their eyes and they embraced Georgie.

"Georgie, don't you worry about Hope, I will stay with her okay?"

"Oh Grandma, I can't ask you to do that, you just got moved in by Mom and Dad."

"Wait a minute," interrupted Cindy, "Hope lived alone before and we will be over there a lot.

She will be just fine but Mom, you must report to the recruiting office tomorrow."

"Would you come with me Dad?"

"Sure! When you're ready to go, come and pick me up alright?"

"How am I going to tell Hope Mom?"

"We will find a way. You and Hope have been very close and I know she will miss you and so will we."

George walked over to his Grandma and gave her a hug. "I will miss you Grams."

"I will miss you too Georgie," as they both shed tears.

"I will see you before I go Grams. I love you." As he said goodbye to Cindy and Peter, he said "see you in the morning Dad."

When he got home it seemed so quiet, he sat in the kitchen thinking, when would he have to leave? Where would they send him? How would Hope feel and oh what about Jenny?

"Hello George is that you?"

"Yes, Jenny, can I come over? Is it too late?"

"Sure Geroge come on over." She was happy to hear his voice. George couldn't stay home as he was too upset from the news he had gotten. He had to talk to someone. He had gotten a ring for Jenny but wasn't sure if he should give it to her now or not. Maybe she might not accept it since he was going into the army. As he drove over to her place, he was debating if he should or not. As he knocked on the door, she greeted him with a hug and a kiss.

"I am glad to see you George," she said. "We have both been so busy, come on in. I have some coffee," and sat down beside George. "Are you okay?"

"Well, I … I have something to tell you." He hesitated to say anything when a soft voice came to him and said, "George don't be afraid, she loves you." George heeded the voice and then he turned to Jenny. He knew it was God speaking to his heart. As he turned to Jennifer he pulled out the letter and gave it to her.

"What is this honey? You mean…"

"Yes, Jen, I have to report to the recruiting office in the morning."

"Oh George, I don't know what to say."

"Jen, I have another question I want to ask you, but you have to let me know about the letter and how you feel."

"What do you mean George?" she asked.

He pulled out a small delicate box and gave it

to her, watching her expression as she opened it. "Will you marry me, Jennifer?"

She was stunned by the question and George said, "you can let me know or think about it."

"What about the Army?"

"We can live on base if that's okay." He took the ring out of the box, looked at Jen and took her hand. "This is to tie us together."

Jennifer accepted the engagement ring. "It's beautiful George, what do you think about marrying when you finish your training. That will give us both time to prepare for the wedding."

"That will be great Jenny…. I love you and will see you before I leave. I will see you tomorrow night." He gave her a big hug and they kissed passionately. George didn't want to leave her, but he needed to get back before Hope got home. She had been working at the church late and would be tired. When he drove in the driveway, he knew Hope was home because the light was on, but he would wait and tell her when they were by Dad's. She met him at the door as he came in.

"Where were you?" she asked. "I thought you would be in bed."

"No… I went to see Jennifer for awhile. Hope! I gave her a ring tonight and she accepted.

I asked her to marry me and she said yes." He couldn't wait to tell her.

"George! That's wonderful, when is the big day? Did you set the date?"

"Well..not exactly. Oh, by the way, I need to leave early tomorrow I have some place to go."

"George, are you stopping at the school first?"

"Why? Is something wrong?"

"Oh no," replied Hope, "I just wondered."

"See you in the morning. Hope… come here a minute please."

Hope wondered why, "what is it George?"

"Can we pray together like Mom and Dad do before calling it a day?"

"Sure George, that would be nice."

As she came down the steps, George saw a frail young lady and wasn't ready to tell her what was going to happen. He and Hope sat near the fireplace and opened the Bible to a verse that said, "blessed are the peacemakers for they shall inherit the earth." And Hope read the rest, and then together they prayed a prayer of comfort and love for God, that he will watch over each other. And George told Hope to be sure and eat when she should and don't over work.

"When Jenny and I get married, we want you to be maid of honor, okay, but listen we will talk about it later. I have to meet Dad in the morning on some business, so you have a good night."

He caressed her as she did him and turned the lights off and walked upstairs together.

"See you in the morning bro," Hope said.

"Good night sis," George said. As he went to his room, he sat on the bed and thought, "is this what God has in mind for me, his plans are not always what we want." He couldn't sleep, so he got the bible out and read until he got sleepy. The next morning, was a big day for him, he had to report to the recruiting office but what would they tell me?

Hope and George had breakfast together and then left to do what they had to do. George left to pick up Peter and asked his mother if she would like to come. "I would love to son." She and Peter never dreamed they would lose their son to the Army, but if that was God's calling, they would accept it.

"Did you tell Hope son?"

"No, I would like to tell her after I see the officer. Then you and Dad can go with me, okay?"

"Sure son, I think that's a good idea. We'll

take her out for lunch and then tell her, but don't worry she will be fine."

As they drove to the recruiting office, they were very quiet and Georgie finally agreed everything would be fine. He would accept God's calling whatever it was. He would have courage and faith as he had been taught by his parents and as he has taught the boys at the Christian School. When they arrived, they met the officer and he began with how George was and what type of work he was doing and many other questions.

"Officer, where will he be stationed?" asked Peter.

"First he will be training in Fort Monical, and then they will go to Reiner Base in Germany. Your son is a good trainer to the boys, so he may be good at training new recruits. It depends upon where they need him."

"When I go," asked George, "I need to let the school know."

"Don't worry son, Cindy and I will take care of the school. We will need to find a new coach until you come back."

"Well, you must report to Fort Monical base one week from today, and you will need to have a physical before you go," said the Officer.

"Yes sir," replied George.

"So, here are your papers to take with you to the doctors."

As they stood up, Officer Hagan shook George's hand and wished him good luck, and then shook hands with Peter and Cindy. "We are proud to have your son with us."

They all left, not saying too much as they went to pick up Hope for lunch. She had been working at the school for the young group. She enjoyed her work very much. "Hi Mom! Hi Dad! Where are we going?"

She looked at George and did not mention the wedding. "Well," said Cindy, "we're just going to stop to eat and we thought it would be nice for you to come too."

As they got to the diner, George said to Cindy, "Mom you tell her."

"Tell me what?" Hope asked. "Dad what is it?"

"Hope, Georgie got a letter from the Army."

"What for? I have been drafted in the Army Hope," he said it very slowly to not upset Hope.

"What! You're going into the service? When, Georgie?"

I have to report to Fort Monical base in Indiana one week from today for training."

"Oh no! What … what about Jennifer? I thought…" and she stopped. So surprised at the news she didn't know what to say. "George, did you tell Mom and Dad the other news?"

"No… but since we are together it will be a good time."

"Tell us what dear?" Cindy asked.

"I have asked Jenny to marry me!"

"You did?" asked Peter. "What did she say?"

"She said yes! After I finish my training and I come home on a pass, that way it will give her time to prepare for the wedding. Then we can live on base together."

"Do Jenny's parents know George? They were in bed so Jenny was going to tell them. Grandma doesn't know yet." As they cheered him on his engagement, they were sad about losing him to the Army but God chose him for a reason so he must serve and now they had a new daughter.

"Georgie, do you think Mom and I could give Jenny a party?" Cindy thought that would be great, but they wanted to spend as much time with George as they could before he left. Hope was so surprised by all the news she said she had to get back to work so she wouldn't break into tears.

They took Hope back to the school, and Georgie went so he could talk to John and Jerry. They would be a big help to Peter while George was gone. Cindy and Peter met with the staff and everyone was surprised and would miss George a lot.

"We need to find someone to coach the boys while he is gone," replied Pastor Olson.

"Wait..." Pastor said, "John you took coaching in college didn't you?"

"Yes, but I never used it."

"Would you like to work with me this week before I leave?" George asked.

"Well, what about Jerry? He will need help with the boys."

"He will have plenty of help," said Peter. "Cindy and I will be here and mother love's helping them when she can. Jerry will have lots of help. Remember I am not preaching at this time, but God will help us at all times when we ask him too. I may be assisting at the church but I will be here everyday with Jerry and we will find someone to help him also."

"Sure George," replied John. "I would love to coach the boys."

"Thank You!"

John was happy about the decision as he returned to help Jerry.

George prepared for the upcoming week of leaving and Peter got back to the promise he made Mike, the young boy he found on the side of the road. He was to meet him the same weekend that Georgie was to leave for training. He turned to Cindy and Lynda and said, "this has been a surprising week hasn't it Mom? But with God's grace we will find. I also told the police officer in Shiloh, that I would visit Mike this weekend. I haven't heard from them yet. I hope it is okay. He was so looking forward to coming home with us. I know he would like it here, but if he is happy, we won't disturb him."

"Why don't we call back in the morning and find out?" Lynda asked.

"Good idea," replied Cindy as they drove home in silence.

As the week passed, the school had given George a farewell party and congratulated him and Jennier on their engagement. Peter and Cindy along with Grandma Lynda drove George to the airplane and were sad to see him go. They gave a hug and wished him God's blessings.

The following day, Lynda stayed by Hope

because it was difficult for both of them to be alone. George was gone and Peter and Cindy were going to see Mike for the weekend. Hope and Lynda were planning a wedding shower for Jenny. They hadn't met her parents yet.

"Grandma, wouldn't it be nice if you and I went over to meet Jenny's folks?" asked Hope.

"That would be nice Hope, because no one has met them yet. I have met Jenny and she is a very nice girl."

So, while Peter and Cindy drove to Shiloe to see Mike and George had left after saying goodbye to Jenny as she was holding back tears, Lynda and Hope called Jenny's parents and asked if they would come over to see them and if Jennifer was home. Mr. and Mrs. Davis were surprised at the phone call because they wanted to get together with George's family.

"Sure Miss Watkins, I would love to meet Georgie's family. He is such a vibrant and honest young man. Why don't you two come for supper? Jenny will be home also."

"Oh, thank you. Grams and I will see you and six o'clock, bye bye." Hope hung up and told Lynda that they were invited to supper at Jenny's house at six.

"That will be an honor," said Lynda. Lynda looked forward to meeting the Davis's. Hope and Lynda went to the Davis's and introduced themselves as did Mr. and Mrs. Davis. "I am Anna and this is my husband Arthur. We are very glad to meet you both. We were sorry to see George go into the service, but we know that God chose the time and place for all of us."

Hope and Lynda felt very comfortable with Jenny and her family. They had a good meal and then Anna asked Hope if they had any questions they had on their mind. Hope said, "yes, we would like to give Jenny a shower if it's alright."

"Jennier would you like that?" asked Mrs. Davis.

"I would love it. George won't be home for six weeks from basic training."

Of course it was mostly women talk, so Arthur excused himself. The three ladies didn't discuss too much in front of Jenny. She had some school papers to correct so she went to do that. The other three would get together again and decide when, where, and other details the following Saturday.

"Thank you so much Anna for having us for supper. It was nice to meet you both and we will see you Saturday."

Lynda had made a new friend and could spend time with Anna. Anna and Arthur didn't go to Peter's church but that didn't matter. God is everywhere!

Peter and Cindy had driven to Shiloe to see Mike, so Hope and Lynda would fill Cindy in when they got home. When they got to Shiloh, they stopped at the police department to get the address where Mike was staying. When they arrived there, Mike was waiting for them outside. As they got out of the car, Mike ran to Peter.

"Hi Peter! You, you did keep your promise. Hi Cindy!"

"Why sure we did," Peter and Cindy were just as glad to see Mike as Mike was to see them. Mr and Mrs. Watkins walked Mike to the house and the lady of the house invited them in. She introduced herself as Mrs. Stratton. "Mike has been a very good boy. We love him like our own."

"We are happy to hear that," replied the Watkins. "He was so unhappy when we found him that we just wanted to take him home with us. Mike, are you happy here? You sure look like it."

"Yes, Mr. Watkins, Mrs. Stratton and Mr. Stratton are great parents. God has given me a good home finally. Can you stay and go to church with us tomorrow? Can they Mom?" Mike asked.

"Well we don't want to be a bother."

"That's no trouble," said Mrs. Stratton.

"We will get a room at the hotel and meet you here in the morning. Oh, Mike, would you like to go for an ice cream treat?" asked Cindy.

"Can I Mom? Can I?" asked Mike. "I can show them where the church is."

"Alright, but don't be gone for long. Doug will be home soon and they can meet him and stay for supper."

"Okay!" All excited, Mike went with the Watkins and enjoyed the ice cream. He showed Peter where the hotel was. After having supper they decided that it was time to call it a day and would see them in the morning for church.

On Sunday, Peter and Cindy met Mike and the Stratton's and followed them to the church and then they all stopped for lunch. They thanked the Strattons for letting them see Mike and giving him something that the boy needed - love, a home, and someone who cares. Mike seemed very happy, so that made Peter and Cindy satisfied and gave Mike a hug and wished him much love and happiness.

"Thank you Peter," said Mike.

"Thanks for coming, Mike had turned into a boy that anyone would be glad to have."

Peter and Cindy said goodbye to all of them and were on their way home. They enjoyed riding on the country roads, seeing all the scenery and animals feeding in the pastures. "Cindy! Wouldn't it be nice to take the boys on a field trip so see all the animals and how they grow into adults, cows and chickens? Some of them have never been on a farm. What do you think dear?"

"I, I think they would love that! It would be a change for them too."

"We can discuss it with the staff and see how many would like to go," Peter said. As he drove, he continued to admire God's work and the beautiful colors he creates.

Being a minister, he wanted to do God's work and teaching the boys about nature was a part of letting them know how and what he created. This would be his way of helping God do what's needed to be done. They were finally home and glad to be back.

Lynda was there sitting by the window when she saw them drive up. She went to open the door and was relieved that they were okay. "Home safe," she said! "How was your trip son? Cindy?"

"It went very well Mom, Mike is very happy isn't he Cindy? He has a new family who loves him and treats him with love and care."

"He goes to church with them?"

"Yes Mom! I can say he is going to be fine. We had a good visit."

"I am glad to hear that," Lynda said.

They put the suitcases in the bedroom and sat in the living room relaxing from the long trip. As the night fell upon them, they watched the sun go down, red and beautiful as God could ever make it. "Have you ever seen a more beautiful painting?" asked Cindy.

"No dear! It is one of our heavenly fathers'."

The following morning, Lynda had coffee on and Cindy came out and helped fix breakfast. As they all three sat and had coffee, Lynda asked them if they had plans.

Peter asked, "why Mother? Is there somewhere you need to go? You can come to the church if you would like."

"Well...I ... need to talk to Cindy if she isn't really busy."

"Sure Mom, I can stay for awhile and talk, that's alright Peter, isn't it?"

"That's okay, I will go ahead and let you two

wonderful ladies do your talking," he kissed them both and left.

Cindy and Lynda cleaned the table and finished the dishes. "Okay Mom, what would you like to talk about?"

"Well, you know your son George is getting married after his basic training."

"Sure Mom, we are happy for him."

"Well", said Lynda, "Hope and I and of course you are planning a wedding shower for Jennifer. What do you think of that Cindy?"

"Mom, I think that's a grand idea. We can have it here if that's okay. We have plenty of room."

"Well... Cindy, I think Jennifer's Mom plans to have it there, I'm not sure. You and she can decide that."

"Does Hope want to help?" asked Cindy.

"Oh sure! It was her idea," replied Lynda. "We are all four meeting on Saturday at seven. Can you make it?"

"I will be there," Cindy replied. "Oh! Where are we meeting?"

"Well, why don't we meet here?"

"Okay," replied Lynda, "we will call Anna, Jennifer's Mom and Hope, and let them know."

"Oh Mom! This will be so exciting. George

will like to know our families are getting to know each other. I better go to school Mom. Would you like to come along?"

"No dear, I guess I will stay here and do some work."

"Alright Mom, I will see you later."

After Cindy left, Lynda did some dusting and vacuuming. She was thinking about George, she was wondering how he was and how his training was coming along. She missed having him and Hope around. They were always there when she needed someone. "Would Hope be okay by herself?" she wondered. She continued straightening beds and then called Anna, Jen's mother.

"Hello?" said a soft, gentle voice, said Jenny on the phone.

"Jennifer, this is Georgie's grandmother, how are you? May I speak to your mother?" As Jennifer called Anna to the phone, Lynda wondered if they had heard from George. Anna and Lynda talked awhile and planned to meet by Cindy and Peter's on Saturday to discuss the shower plans trying to keep most of it a secret.

No one had heard from Geroge yet. He had six weeks before he could come home. Phone calls and letters were allowed certain times. He had only been there one week when George finally wrote a letter to say that he was okay and they have a little chapel to go to church. The sergeant had made him a captain of the squad. "Tell Jennie I will write or call her tomorrow," in his closing. He wrote, "I miss all of you, but will be back before you know it. Take care of Hope and Grams. Till next time, I love you, Dad and Mom. All my love, your son George Jr.."

Hope had stopped to see if they had any news from George. "Dad has George wrote yet?" Hope asked.

"Yes, sweetheart," Peter said. "We will read it together after supper if that's okay. You will stay for supper, won't you Hope?"

"Sure Dad, and then I have a practice at the church at 7:00 o'clock."

Peter had called Jennifer and invited her over the phone. "Thank you Mr. Watkins," she said. "I can't wait to hear from him. Tell Hope that I will meet her at the church."

"I will," said Peter. "Bye Bye."

Hope and the family were glad to hear that George was okay and Jenny couldn't wait till George was home on a pass. She and her parents were saving for the wedding. They were all excited about it. As time passed, Hope and Cindy and Mrs. Davis had invited many people from both sides of the families at the shower. Hope couldn't believe that her twin brother was going to get married. How exciting that is going to be. The three had the shower a week before it was time for George to come home. When he came home, they would get married and she would go back with him. Now that the shower was over, they had many things to do for the wedding. Peter and Cindy called the church and made arrangements, but had to ask Jenny what she thought at first.

"Jennifer, Cindy and I talked to the church staff and if you don't mind, I would be honored to be the pastor to marry you and George."

Jennifer looked at her parents and they smiled with joy and happiness. "That's wonderful," they replied and shook hands. "Thank you Peter," said Arthur, Jenny's Dad. They had many plans. Since Anna and Arthur were the bride's parents, they decided along with Jenny that they would have the dinner at their house. It was the first wedding for both families. Jennifer had written to George and asked who he chose for the best man and his groomsmen. Hope was maid of honor and George chose John for his best man and Jerry for his groomsmen. They were close as brothers could be. They always helped George and Peter when necessary. Jenny would pick the bridesmaids.

George only had a week before he'd return to his post in Maine. That would be where he and Jenny would be living, but she would be alone often while George was out with the troops for field training. The week went by fast for Jenny and Geroge and the wedding went of beautiful. Tears were shed by the parents. They were losing their oldest child, but wished them both good luck. Hope invited them to stay with her as she would have a big house to herself. When they were ready to catch the plane back to Camp Reiner Base in Germany, everyone gave hugs to them and yelled out to them, we love you both and waved goodbye till they were out of sight. Cindy and Peter talked to John and Jerry and said they did a good job.

"We were happy to be part of it Mr. Watkins. Thank you and George for asking us to be part of it all."

After all had settled down to its normal routine,

Peter and Cindy went to the Crhistian school and Peter was introduced to the new boy's that had come in while they were gone to Shiloh to see Mike. One was called Danny and his brother Eric. Peter asked the boys "where did you live before?"

"Well," replied Eric, the oldest son, "our home is in Rome, Georgia, but our father died and our mother is working, so we were left alone most of the time."

"Are you and Danny okay with being here?" asked Peter.

"It's okay," said Danny. Not sure how long he would be there. John asked the boys if they would like to join the baseball team. Eric smiled and was all excited. "I do," he said. "I love to play baseball."

Danny wasn't sure about that. He was shy and quieter than Eric, so he didn't say anything. "What about you Danny?" John asked. "Don't you want to play ball?"

"No! I don't want to be here," he answered.

"Why not?" asked Peter. Peter knew this type of boy. God had saved him from poverty and loneliness and that's what he wanted for all the boys that came to his school, you know what that's what he wanted for all the boys that came to his school.

"You know what Danny?" Peter took his hand

and walked down the hall with him. "Let's sit here for a while so we can talk."

"About what?" said Danny.

"Well, about your Mom, where she works and how did your Dad die? Maybe it will help you to talk about it."

Peter and Danny sat outside where Peter could tell him about how he was a boy and had to lean on God to get him through the times when his Mom and Dad died.

"My Mom is a nurse at the hospital," replied Danny. "My Dad was sick for a long time, Mom said he had a bad heart and after the funeral, she had a hard time keeping up the rent."

"So, that's why you and Eric came her?"

"Yes sir, we didn't know where to go and Mom brought us here. Eric likes it but I don't."

"Why not Danny?" asked Peter.

"Because I miss my Dad. He didn't have to die." Tears running down.

"No, Danny, he didn't have to die, but God had called him home with him and he's watching over you and Eric from heaven."

"Can he see us and hear us? And where is heaven, who is God?" Danny had many questions for Peter.

"Well first of all, God is our father in heaven. He watches over everyone and when he thinks it the time for us to go with him, we are in his house which is heaven. And yes, Danny, I believe your Dad can see you and Eric and he wants you to be happy because when you are sad, he gets sad. Do you know what I am saying, Danny?"

"I guess so, Mr. Watkins."

"Let's fold our hands son and say a prayer, okay?" Peter prayed, "dear Lord, protect these two young boys, Eric and Danny, and bless their mother who loves them. Give the body faith and courage that they may know you love them and teach them in the way you would have them go, Amen. Well, Danny, are you ready to go in by Eric?"

"Okay," said Danny as he took Peter's hand and walked with him quietly. Danny and Peter joined the rest of the boys who were doing their own thing at rest time. Some were reading and others were playing games. Eric was by the older boys who were getting ready to practice ball with George.

"Will you stay with me Peter?" Danny asked.

"Sure, Danny, what would you like to do? How about this group that are playing games? They look like they are having fun." Peter sat down with Danny and the other boys until Danny got to be comfortable playing with the other boys. "Well Son, I must be going, I have another appointment. You all have met Danny so make him feel welcomed."

Danny joined me and was glad to meet one boy his age and they both had lost their Dads so they had something in common to talk about. He and Eric shared their room together and at night time when they were alone, they talked about their Mom and Dad and how much God has helped them get through bad things and how Peter and Cindy cared for all the boys in God's house. Even though they were of different ages, they understood each other.

The next day, Peter wondered how George was and why hasn't he heard from them. He wasn't used to not being able to call his son and now there was Jenny. "Were they both okay?" he wondered. Putting it in God's hands, he knew they would hear from them soon. Cindy was busy helping Lynda. Peter called out, "Cindy, Mother, I am leaving for the church. I will see you both for supper."

"Goodbye George … We mean Peter," they said. George had been on their minds also. They also had a busy day planned. They were off to see how things were at the Christian boys school.

The children were all getting ready for breakfast and the pastor was leading the prayer. The day consisted of bible classes and the regular school teachings. Some boys need special help, so Mrs. Johnson helped those who were slow at learning and of course Hope would have her daily singing with everyone, and then choir practice after hours. She was also worried about George and Jenny. After the school day ended, she stopped by her Mom and Dad's to see if they had heard anything.

"Hi Dad, Mom, hello Grams. Have you heard anything from Georgie and Jenny?"

"We finally did dear," they replied. "He and Jenny are fine and Jenny has made friends on the base."

"How are you Hope?" Cindy asked.

"Well," said Hope, "I sure miss them. The house seems so empty at night. I miss you too Grams. I guess I will get used to it."

Peter and Cindy didn't like the idea of her living alone at night. "Maybe we can find someone in church that would share the house with you," said Cindy.

"That would be a great Mom."

"Meanwhile, why don't you spend a couple of nights with us? We would be glad to have you here."

"We can get together and sing songs," replied Grandma. "Is that alright Peter?" She loved sitting by the fire and singing.

"Of course it is," he said, "anytime dear. There's always a place for you and George. When grandpa was living, he would never let you out of his sight Hope.

"I sure miss him a lot," Hope relied. "I can remember when he stayed with me in the hospital and read to me till I fell asleep and then kissed me on the cheek and said sweet dreams."

"You were his pride and joy, Hope, he loved his whole family so much. When we found Peter, his whole life changed. He was finally the way he dreamed it would be. The school and the boys were his life until we found Peter, you are a gift from God and you and Cindy have given us two wonderful grandchildren."

"Mother," said Peter, "Dad and you are the best thing that could have happened to me. Mother Glenis had said, someone would take care of me that was chosen by God. Those were her last words and he did find or choose you and Dad. He chose good Christian people. Thanks be to God for that. Well, Hope dear, should we gather and you can play the piano while we all sing?"

"Sure Dad, lets go."

They sang "Amazing Grace" and listened to the children singing and last "Sweet Hour of Prayer" afterwards they were ready to call it a night. Cindy showed Hope the guest room. Grandma was much relieved that Hope wasn't going to be alone.

Hope stayed with them for a few days until Peter found a young lady to share the house with her. The following week, Hope helped the young lady move in and gave her a tour of the house. Her name was Mary Schultz. She taught Sunday school at the church. They made a good pair. Hope and she became good friends. She told her about her family and where she had lived before she moved to Rome, Georgia. She couldn't understand why Hope couldn't eat the same things she ate. One day at supper time, Mary asked Hope about her diet. "Hope, why can't you eat regular food and drink regular milk? Is there something I can help you with?"

"Oh no Mary, I'm doing fine. See when I was born, I was diagnosed with P.O.E, or protein deficiency. Too much protein and was in the hospital for quite a while because my protein was too high and they said I might not make it or I may be disabled. So, they put me on special formula and a diet for the rest of my life, that's why I can't eat the same foods as you."

"I am so sorry Hope! I didn't mean to pry into your private life," said Mary.

"Oh, that's okay Mary, you didn't know and it's best that you do. Then if I get sick or have a seizure, you will know who to call. I haven't had one for quite a while. Thank God for that. That's why my Mom and Dad didn't want me to live alone."

"I do understand," said Mary. "I am glad you told me."

The two of them talked for hours that night about their families and their work. They didn't realize how late it was until Hope started getting sleepy and said, "Oh Mary, I think we better say goodnight if we are going to get up for work in the morning."

"Oh my! Is it that late?" asked Mary. "I guess you are right."

They walked to their separate rooms and

said goodnight to each other. "See you in the morning," said Hope.

Mary wasn't only a Sunday school teacher she was a nurse at Willis Knight Medical Hospital in Rome, Georgia. So, they both had a busy career. Mary worked in the pediatrics area and loved them all. Hope and she had a lot in common. They both worked with children.

As the week went by, the family waited for word from George. It always made them feel better to know he was well and okay. Jenny would write often to her parents and the two families would exchange information. Anna, Cindy, and Lynda had become good friends. They enjoyed each other's company. Unlike some in-laws, they could talk about their children and not feel jealous that one was better than the other ones. Peter and Arthur also got along, but didn't see each other as often as the ladies did. Arthur would say how he wished he had a son to carry on the family tradition even though they loved Jennifer very much. Peter was still keeping up with his Dad's dream at the school. It meant the world to him and Lynda. He worried about his mother a lot. He didn't want to lose her like he did his mother Glennis. Sometimes, memories come back to him and how sick his mother was.

Thinking of Lynda, he called her to see how she was. "Mom, are you okay?"

"Sure Peter! Why do you ask?"

"Well, I was just thinking of Mother Glennis and I couldn't help thinking of you."

"Oh Son! I, I am fine but thank you dear for calling."

"I love you, Mom," Peter said.

"I love you too," Lynda replied.

"See you later Mom, bye." As he hung up, he felt better but left Lynda with a sad feeling for Peter. How could she or what could she do to make him feel better? She decided she would ask him to take her to the cemetery Sunday after church. Maybe seeing and talking to his mother and Dad, even though she knew he loved her and Geroge Sr. It was Friday night when Peter came home from school. The family was together except George. Lynda asked Peter at the supper table, "Peter would you mind taking me to the cemetery after church Sunday? I haven't been there for a while and you can stop to see your parents also. Sometimes we need to talk to them and let them know we didn't forget them, and it makes us feel better to know they are in God's hands. Hope would you like to go?" she asked.

"I would like to go see grandpa and Mary, Cindy's Mom. Oh, also your other Mom and Dad," Hope replied.

"Good," said Cindy. "We will all meet for lunch out and then take a ride to the cemetery. It will be a good family day."

"Sounds great Mom," said Peter. "We should do this every Sunday."

"You're right dear," said Lynda.

The day had gone very well. Peter did feel better after spending time at the cemetery, talking to his father George Sr and his real parents. God had let him know everything was going to be okay. Lynda was in her late seventies but doing well. She had a little trouble walking but wouldn't use a wheelchair. She wouldn't give up and that's why Peter had worried about losing her also. God had assured him that his Mom would be okay. Peter loved Lynda very much. How could he ever repay her and Dad for taking him in as their own son? They were such wonderful parents. She was his main concern right now but always thought of Hope and George. His family was his whole life, and yet he gave all he could to the church and cared about all the boys at the Christian Boy School. Some of them needed more attention than others. As usual, when they got a new student, they would have trouble getting them to stay. Peter went after him and was gentle as he spoke about how his Dad died and it was very important to see him at the funeral and say goodbye. He told the young boy, that God takes care of us all when we go to heaven. This seemed to satisfy the young boy and he told his brother and Mom. Danny had made many friends after that and adjusted to the school very well. Peter was proud of all the boys and he knew his father Geroge was also.

Weeks passed and they hadn't heard from Georgie. Peter and Cindy became concerned. "Peter," said Cindy, "has Aruthur or Anna mentioned anything of Jennifer or George?"

"No dear, I haven't heard anything. I'm sure they are alright. Sometimes they are out on a maneuver and can't write."

"Well, what about Jenny?"

"I'm sure she would let us know if anything was wrong dear."

"Well, I guess you're right," replied Cindy, but she still couldn't help wondering why they didn't write.

It was evening and she and Grandma picked up the Bible and turned it to a verse that caught their eye. "Fear not for the Lord is with you." Reading that Cindy's fears were released because she knew God would take care of George.

A week later, Cindy had gotten a phone call from the army base where Geroge was stationed. She didn't want to hear bad news, so she called Peter from the other room to take the call. "What is it Cindy?" he asked.

"I don't know, it's, it's from the army base."

Peter took the phone and the officer explained that George was going to be transferred to a new base and wouldn't have time to let his folks know.

"Well, what about his wife?" Peter asked. "What is she going to do?"

"She doesn't want to stay here by herself and she can't get a hold of her parents," replied the officer.

"I think they are on vacation out of town this week," answered Peter. "Is there anything we can do for her?"

"Maybe there is. I will have her contact you and you can let her know about her parents. Maybe you can help her get home while George is gone," said the office.

"I will do the best I can. Please! Have her call, okay?" said Peter, "and thank you for calling us sir."

Cindy and Peter were very worried about Jennifer. "Why didn't Geroge let me know he was being moved?"

"Darling, what, what are we going to do?"

"We will wait for Jennie's call and then fly out and bring her home."

The next day, after the officer had reached Jennifer and gave her Peter's phone number, she called them and was happy to hear their voices. She had been crying and Peter could tell by the sound of her voice. "Jenny! What is wrong?" he asked.

"Mr. Watkins, I... I don't want to stay here alone. George has been transferred. It was all unexpected to Germany."

"Jenny, it's alright. The officer called us and we want to help you if we can."

"Where did Mom and Dad go, do you know?" asked Jenny.

"No, they didn't say," replied Peter. "Can you get a ticket here?" he asked.

"I don't think so," she said. "I will check with the Captain and let you know right away."

"If you can't Jenny, we will send the tickets to

you alright and we will meet you at the airport. Call us back right away, okay dear?"

Jenny was at the captain's quarters and when she hung up she asked the captain where she could get the tickets to fly back home. "Let me check with my superior and find out," he replied.

"Oh thank you sir, I'll wait."

The captain checked with Major Stern and he okayed the ticket for Jenny to get home safe. "Jennife,"r said the captain, "Major Stern has paid everything for your way home. Your tickets will be here soon. If you have anything to do, you may get it. Oh! We will notify George of your returning home."

"Thank you, Captain, I feel so much better now." She hugged him and went to gather her things and waited for the tickets. Meanwhile, she knew Peter was waiting to hear how things were going, so she called Peter and Cindy. Cindy answered the phone and was glad to get the call.

"Jenny, are you okay?" she asked.

"Oh yes, Cindy, I am now. The captain has been so kind and has helped me to get tickets to come home."

"That's great! I am so glad. I'll let you talk to Peter okay?"

She handed the phone to Peter and Jenny explained the situation to him. "The Major Stern had set things up for me to return home tonight. It will be a late flight Peter," she said.

"That will be okay Jenny, you can stay with us tonight. I will pick you up at the airport," he said. She had never flown on a plane before.

"Thank you, Peter! Well, I better get my things together and get to the airport. I will see you later Peter."

"Jenny," he replied, "have a safe trip!"

When she was ready to leave the staff sergeant handed her the ticket to fly home The Army will always take care of their people.

As she boarded the plane, she thought of how much she missed George and that saying goodbye was not easy. As she sat down in her seat, she leaned back and closed eyes and when she awoke, she didn't know what was happening. She muttered out loud, "what what's happening?" and she tried to stand to look around to see what was going on but was suddenly pushed back into her seat.

The person next to her had told her not to move. "What's happening?" she cried. "Where are we?"

"It's a hi-jacking ma'am. They want the pilot to turn the plane around and fly them to another country."

"Terrorists?" she asked nervously.

"I'm not sure," came the reply next to her.

"Oh dear God," she prayed, "don't let them hurt anyone."

"I, I'm afraid it's too late for that lady. They have already killed two passengers," spoke one other passenger.

"What can we do?" Jennifer asked.

"Just do what we say," replied the stewardess. "We have two undercover agents on the plane. We're counting on them to take care of the problem."

As the plane circled, it suddenly dipped sharply to the right and the passengers screamed wondering what was going on as the undercover agents dashed to the front of the plane. With the help of several other brave men, they took two of the hi-jackers down, and a stewardess pulled open the pilot's cabin causing the third hi-jacker to lose his balance and give the co-pilot and the stewardess a chance to knock him out and take him out of the cabin and tie him up. Everyone cheered and the pilot radioed to the law that they would be landing shortly to bring in three hi-jackers.

"Well done," replied a voice from the other end. "Very smart job done."

After they landed, and it was time to take off again, some refused to get back on the plane and others called friends and relatives. Jennifer had called George first, as he had heard of the hi-jacking and was glad to hear she was okay. He assured her that she would be alright now, "thank God," he said.

"Well, you must board the plane George, your Dad and Mom are picking me up at midnight. I miss you darling, I hope you're doing okay and I love you, bye bye."

"Bye dear," replied George. "I will call you tomorrow honey," he said.

Jenny had also called Peter and Cindy to let them know that she would be late and what had happened on the plane. As Jennifer boarded the plane again, she relaxed and knew that she would be alright because God had helped them through the terror. The passengers thanked the stewardess and the pilots for keeping them safe and a job well done. They continued their flight in a quiet night and were happy that God had sent protection for them. As the plane landed in the little town of Rome, Georgia, the passengers were delighted to be home or at their destination. Family and friends picked them up and made sure that they were okay. Peter and Cindy stood waiting for Jenny, and Hope had rode along with them even though she had to go to work the next day. It was more important to know that Jennifer was alright. As they watched her get off the plane, they waived their hands so she would see where they were. She ran over to them and they embraced her as though she had been their own daughter. They made her feel very welcomed.

Tears came to their eyes, "I don't know how to thank you all. Are Mom and Dad home from vacation yet?" she asked.

"No, Jenny, I'm sure they are having a good vacation, but I am very surprised they hadn't called or let you know where they are," said Peter.

"We'll will track them down and make sure they are okay, but for now," as they drove home from the airport, "let's just go home and get some rest and tomorrow is a new day. Things will look brighter."

Dad said, "Hope is it alright if Jenny and I stay here tonight?"

"Oh! You sure can! We have plenty of room.

Grandma is probably sound asleep, so try to be quite alright?"

When they arrived at home, they were very quiet and ready to call it a day.

"Well," said Peter, "let's pray together before we hit the pillows."

They clasped hands and Peter prayed. "Oh Father! We have so much to thank you for, we are thankful for getting Jenny home safe and that the other passengers are safe. Lord, we also pray for our son George who is in Germany to do the best he can for you and to come home safely when time is up. We pray for Jenny's parents that we may hear a word or a sign that they are alright and safe, Amen."

After their prayer, they went to their rooms and as tired as anyone could be, they were asleep as soon as their heads hit the pillow.

The following morning, Lynda had arisen early to find Hope and Jenny in the next room sound asleep yet. She slipped into the kitchen wondering what to prepare for breakfast. She decided to mix up a batter to make pancakes for all of them. She made coffee and the aroma must have worked for Peter and Cindy.

"Good Morning, Mother," they said.

Lynda said, "good morning kids. How is everything? I see Jenny and Hope are here."

"Yes Mom, they decided to stay the night because it was so late when we got home. I'm sure Jennifer will tell you all about the excitement on the plane. Mom, have you heard anything from Ann and Arthur?"

"No son, but I am sure that they are doing fine and they will be home soon."

A New Arrival

With Georgie in Germany serving his country and God, Peter had to be at the school for the boys more than usual and still help at the church. Jenny and Hope had rose and had breakfast but Jennifer couldn't eat.

"What's wrong Jenny?" asked Hope.

"I, I'm not hungry." She wasn't sure what it was, but thought she might be pregnant. After a few weeks, she knew she was going to have a baby, but didn't tell the family until she had seen the doctor and he confirmed it. His parents had returned home and she told Anna her mother who was very happy.

"Jennifer! You are having a baby? I, we're, going to be grandparents."

"Yes Mom, George doesn't know yet," replied Jenny. "He will be surprised Mom."

Cindy and Peter were surprised. They never dreamed of being grandparents but what a wonderful thing for them. They were getting up in their late 50's now and didn't quite know what to say, until Peter asked if she had told her parents yet.

"They should be so happy."

"Yes, Peter," said Jenny. "I wish Georgie was here. Do you think that he will be happy Cindy?"

"Of course he will be, Dear. He will make a good father and you have a sister in law that's going to spoil it."

Jennifer's parents had noticed how quiet she was but figured it was because George was gone and she missed him, but Jenny was also wondering where Anna and Arthur had gone on their vacation and haven't mentioned it yet.

"Jenny, is something wrong? You are so quiet. Do you feel okay?"

"I'm okay Mom. I just wondered where you and Dad were. I couldn't get a hold of you when I needed you, and Peter and Cindy didn't know where you were either Mom, why didn't you let someone know? If it wasn't for Watkins, I don't know what I would have done."

"Oh darling, we are so sorry. We thought you

would be with Georgie. How long is he going to be in Germany?"

"I'm not sure, Dad, he will call next week and let us know how things are," replied Jenny.

They sat and talked about things they did on their vacation and looked at pictures together until Jennifer got tired.

As the weeks passed, Hope helped to keep Jenny busy so she wouldn't miss George so much. The school was doing fine. Jerry coached the boys and Peter was proud of him and John. Hope and the boys choir sang at a concert and were in first place. Peter knew his Dad would be proud of them all. He went to the church in the morning and to the school in the afternoon. Hope and Jenny were like sisters. When they had time, they did everything together.

One day, Hope asked Jenny if she had done any shopping for the baby yet. "No, I thought it might be too early yet. Mom and Dad want to fix up the baby room."

This made Hope wonder when it would be a good time to have a baby shower for Jenny. Later, as she went to Peter's and Cindy's she asked, "Mom, Grandma, when do you think it would be a good time to give Jennifer a shower?"

"Well," said Cindy, "she's only a few months along, so probably in October, she isn't due till December 12th."

"Can we have one over here Mom?"

"Sure, I think George would like that. We will ask Anna to come."

George had called Peter the following week and was glad to hear that they were watching over the one he loves and couldn't be with. Jenny had told George on the phone that they were going to have a baby. She could hear the joy in his voice on the phone.

"Oh, Jenny, I love you! When is it due?" he asked.

"George, it's due December 12th. The Doctor said that everything is alright so far. Mom and Dad and your folks are very excited about being grandparents. George, how are you? When can you come home?"

"Jenny, I'm fine sweetheart. I will make plans to be home when the baby is due. I don't want to miss a day that God gives us the most precious gift of all. I have to go now dear, I will call you next week. You take care and God bless you all."

Jenny didn't want to hang up but she knew

George had to take care of other soldiers or people. He wasn't a full pledge pastor but he had some training in college and lots from his Dad. She was proud of him. She thought that she had to find something to do to keep her busy and active for the baby. So many things went through her mind, would it be a girl or boy? Would it be healthy? She wondered where she and the baby would live? This would all work out for her and George. She was sure of it. As the months passed and the time had come when Jenny was almost due. She had gotten sick the last few weeks of her pregnancy, but the baby was doing okay. The doctor had told her that she would have to stay in bed for a week.

"What is it doctor?" she asked. "Is the baby alright?"

"Yes," the doctor replied, "but you have what they call consumption. It is a bad lung disease. It is another name for pneumonia. You will have to take lots of fluids and plenty of rest if the baby is to make it."

"Okay doctor, would you ask my Mom to call Peter Watkins and Cindy? He is the pastor and father in-law."

"I certainly will," he said. "Meanwhile, you do

as you should and no getting up except to the restroom."

"Yes doctor, I will."

She had taken her medicine and gradually fell asleep. The doctor had met Anna and Arthur in the other room.

"What's wrong with Jenny doctor?"

"She has consumption and needs to stay in bed. Someone must be home at all times."

"But doctor," Anna had tears in her eyes and Arthur embraced her to comfort her. "What is that?" she asked.

"Well, it's like pneumonia and the lungs can fill up with fluid so you need to keep a lot of fluid in her and here is a prescription. Get her on it as soon as you can."

Jenny's parents were very worried and thought that they better call George but didn't want him to worry, so they waited till they talked to the Watkins who were quite concerned when they got the news.

"May we come and see her, Anna?"

"Well, she is sleeping right now but you can come and it would help to talk to someone. Jenny did tell the doctor to call you both and I'm sure he will."

"Well, we will wait for his call and then come over," said Peter.

"Alright," replied Anna.

The two families got together and prayed that Jenny would be okay. "Is there anything we can do?" asked Cindy. "When did she get sick? Does George know about this?"

"Yes, we called him and he is trying to get a leave of absence so he can be with her."

They were all feeling bad about Jenny and the baby, but all they could do is pray and wait. Peter and Cindy left to stop at the school and see Hope and then home to let Lynda know how things are. She felt bad and hoped that she would get to see her great grandchild. The following day, George had called and said, "Dad, I, I will be home on the weekend. How are things going? Can you pick me up at the airport?"

"Sure Son," replied Peter. "We will be there and Jenny is the same. She doesn't eat much, but her parents take turns staying with her."

"Well Dad, I have to go but I will see you Saturday morning, love you." As they hung up Peter told Cindy and Lynda that George would be home Saturday.

"That's good," said Lynda. "Jenny will be glad

to see him. Maybe it will help her to get well."

"I sure hope so."

As Saturday came and Peter and Cindy went to the airport, they heard the plane was an hour late, so they went to get something to eat while waiting. "Wonder why the plane was so late," said Cindy. "I hope nothing serious is wrong."

"I'm sure it's nothing dear, it is probably a minor problem with it."

The plane finally flew into the airport and as the passengers walked out they saw George in his uniform. "How grown up he looks," replied Cindy. "George!" They called out, "we're over here" and he hurried over by them and gave them both a hug and kissed his Mom on the cheeks.

"I am so glad to see you both," he said. "How is Jenny? Is she better? What about the baby?"

"Well, she is anxious to see you George. We're hoping that she will start getting better when she knows that you're home. Her fever hasn't gone down yet so we need to keep praying for her."

"What about the baby Mom?"

"The doctor said it's okay so far, but she has to eat so the baby can get nourishment."

"Well, let's go over there so you can see for yourself Son."

They arrived at the Davis's home and the doctor had just seen her. "How is she doctor? Can I see her?"

"I'm sure she will be happy to see you George, but she needs her rest so just for awhile." George went in to see Jennie and took her hand in his. She looked at him with tears in her eyes.

"I, I'm sorry darling," she said softly.

"It's alright dear," he said. "You are going to get better and the baby will be fine and healthy, but you must eat something, please Jennie."

"Don't go away George! Stay with me?"

"I will be right here, so you close your eyes."

George sat next to her bed till Jennie fell asleep. Anna looked in on her and checked her fever. Cindy and Peter stayed for awhile till they knew George was going to be alright then they left for home. They told George to call Hope and let her know he was home. When they got home, Lynda was still up waiting to hear how everyone was doing.

"Son, how is George and Jennie? It was getting late and I was getting worried. Is everything okay?"

"George's plane was an hour late Mom," said Peter. "He was glad to be home by Jennie. She still has the fever but George is staying with her."

"Maybe it will give her comfort to know he's home."

"I sure hope so Mom," replied Cindy. "We need to keep praying for her. So before we retire for the night, let's take hands and pray for her and the baby."

As they prayed, they felt something warm go through them and knowing it was God's way of saying Jennie was going to be okay. "I have a feeling our children are going to be just fine," said Lynda. She had this strong feeling. "Somehow we can always tell when God sends us messages in his way. So, you kids get some rest. Tomorrow will be better."

"Okay Mom."

They said goodnight and gave her a hug. It was a sleepless night for everyone. George slept next to Jennie's bed that night and wouldn't leave her side.

"Oh, God," he prayed. "Please make Jennie better and the baby. I promise to do anything you ask of me, but please let them be okay."

It had been two weeks and there was no change in Jennie, but the next morning George went by Jennie's bed and smiled at her because her fever had broke and she was awake. "Anna, Arthur!" he called. "Come, come here."

He was so glad that God had heard his prayer. "Call the doctor," he said. "Jennie, Jennie are you alright? Can you hear me?"

George held her hand and she said, "yes dear, what happened?"

"You were very ill dear, and the doctor said you might not make it."

He gave her a drink of water and told her the baby needed her to get stronger and eat. The doctor arrived shortly and checked Jennie over and listened to the baby's heart beat. It was kind of weak but he had given Mr. and Mrs. Davis instructions to keep her in bed a few more days.

"This is best for her and the baby. It will strengthen them, but George be sure she eats good and rests a lot okay?"

"Sure doctor! I have to be back to camp next week, can she go with me? We have a house that we can all live together."

"Well, I don't know George. At least wait and see how the baby is doing. Do you have a doctor close by? They have both been through a lot."

"Yes, doctor, there is a baby doctor and M.D. that can care for them".

"If she and the baby are ok, when it's time I see no reason why they can't," the doctor said, "but she is due in another month so she needs plenty of rest."

Peter and Cindy had stopped over to see George and Jennie that morning and were very happy to see she was awake. "How is the baby doing?" Cindy asked.

"It's very small, mother, because it hasn't had the correct nourishment but now that Jennie is better, I think it will be fine."

"George let her rest," and he went with his Mom and Dad to see what they thought about Jennie going back with him. "We have a good hospital and we would be together."

"When do you go back son?" Peter asked.

"Next weekend Dad. I hope Jennie will be stronger by then. Is Hope doing alright Mom?"

"Yes dear," replied Cindy. "Why don't you come over for supper tonight and we will call Hope to see if she can come. Grandma's anxious to see you. Hope has been so busy we haven't seen much of her."

"Well, if Anna can stay with Jennie, it would be

nice to be home again," he replied.

"I will ask Anna okay. I am sure she will stay with her."

Hope and George did join their parents and had a good visit with Grandma Lynda who was so worried about Jennie and George. Hope and George had a lot to talk about. They were so excited about the baby. Lynda also, as she was going to have her first great grandchild. She wasn't too well but kept herself busy.

"Dad," said George. "I have decided to become a minister since I have been there for the boys over seas I realize this is what God wanted me to do. What do you think Dad, Mom?"

"Oh George," they embraced him and said, "we couldn't be more proud of you George. When did you decide this?"

Hope looked at George with a surprised look but didn't say anything. She didn't know what to say.

"Hope! What are you thinking? I hope you will be happy for me?" He took her hands and said, "are you alright? Don't you like the idea?"

"I, I'm just so surprised George, but it will be nice to follow in Dad's footsteps. Where will you live?"

"Well, I am not sure yet," he said. "I need to take some college classes first. So, it might be awhile. Sis, I won't forget you! We can talk all the time. I feel I can help people that need someone to talk to. Dad knows what I mean, right Dad?"

"Yes, George," Peter said. "I think it is wonderful."

"What about the boys school?" asked Hope.

"Dad and Mom are here and John and Jerry are old pros by now. You have your music and you love it. You do a wonderful job sis."

"Well, I guess God calls each of us to what he wants us to do," Hope said, "but you just let us know where ever you go and how that baby is doing. I want to be the godmother."

"I wouldn't have anyone else sis." He gave her a hug and said, "I better go now and see how my wife is. Hope, if you're leaving, would you give me a ride home?"

"Sure George, I need to go anyways. I want to stop and see Jennifer."

They said their goodbyes to Cindy, Peter, and of course to Grandma. "I will see you tomorrow, everyone."

They left to go by the Davis's and Hope was surprised to see Jennifer sitting up in bed. "How are you, Jen?" she said. "I was so worried about you and so was everyone else." Hope gave Jennie a hug and said she couldn't wait to see that little bundle come into this world. "What are you going to name it?" she asked.

"Well," said Jennie, "if it's a boy, it will be called George Arthur Watkins and if it's a girl, well, I don't know yet Hope."

"Well George is going to take me home, so I will see you sometime tomorrow. You do what the doctor tells you, alright?"

"I sure will Hope. I don't want to lose the baby now. God has protected it this far and I know he always will."

The next few weeks were crucial for Jennie's baby. Jennie was feeling better and getting stronger. She had decided to wait till the baby was born then join George in Germany where he was stationed. She didn't want to take a chance on traveling. George was disappointed but was very understanding. He was to leave the next day to return to his post but didn't want to leave her alone. "Darling, I must leave tomorrow so you have to take it easy and take care of the baby. I will find us a place to live and when you are stronger, you and the baby can join me. I love you dear!"

"That is so sweet of you George. I can't wait to be back with you. Mom and Dad will help me to get well and your Mom, Dad and Hope will always be there for me."

They spent the night together and Jennie was sad about George leaving by himself the next day. He had to catch the early flight so he kissed her goodbye and left a letter telling her how much he loved her and that he was thinking about becoming a pastor like Peter was. Peter and Cindy were proud to hear that. They took George to the airport the next day and said their goodbyes.

"George," said Cindy, "we will keep in touch with you about how Jennie is doing," as he headed toward the plane.

"Thanks Mom and Dad, I love you. Bye."

They stood and watched the plane till it got out of sight.

When George arrived at his destination, he was greeted by some of his captains and sergeants whom he was close to and had helped him get through some difficult times. Back at base, they had many questions to ask him. "How is your wife and the baby? Why didn't he bring them back with him? Is she alright?"

Questions just kept on coming. Finally

George said, "Wait! I can't answer all at one time. I will answer all of them but first let me get settled in," and he smiled and said, "I'm glad to see you all."

They all waited patiently as George got himself settled in. "First of all, it is a nice welcome back and good to see you all. I had a busy trip, my Mom and Dad picked me up at the airport. I was very worried about Jennie and what I would find when I got to her. She was still unconscious when I arrive and I sat by her side all night and prayed. I asked God to let her be okay and the baby also. The baby was losing ground because Jennie wasn't eating. As I sat there a couple of days, my mother-in-law stayed with her in the daytime so I could get some rest. It was sad to see her suffer like that. The next morning, sitting by her side, I felt a hand on mine and turned to see her open her eyes. She had seen the doctor and he said the worst was over. He said that she was too weak to travel and the baby needed a lot of nourishment. So, my Mom and Dad will send her and the baby home after it is born. It will be a blessed day!"

After the captain and George's friends left, George relaxed and picked up a book to get his mind off of Jennie. He was about to get some sleep when the Colonel came over and reported a soldier was badly hurt and was calling for him. George asked, "who it was and how bad was he?"

"I am not sure," replied the Colonel, "but it sounds pretty bad."

"I will be right there, Sir," said George.

George got ready and grabbed his bible. When he got to the hospital, he had seen many that were wounded and prayed for them. When he came to the one that had asked for him, he looked at him and saw he was really wounded badly. He leaned over by the soldier and asked him, "what is your name, Sir?"

With a soft voice he answered, "Steve Johnson."

"Steve, can I do anything for you?" Steve was hard to hear but he asked George to pray for him. He knew that he wasn't going to make it. George started to pray for him and asked God to watch over Steve and keep him in his care. As George was praying for Steve, Steve passed away. George felt bad and yet he was honored to be of God's help. He had stopped to see a couple other ones also. "Is this how it feels to be a pastor, when they need to do God's work?"

More and more, it made him feel this is God's calling for him. He began to study a little Greek and the books of the bible.

Weeks past and Jennie was almost due with the baby. George walked the floor as the men tried to keep him calm. Until one evening, the Captain's phone rang and it was Peter. "Captain, is George there?"

"Yes sir, he said. I will get him."

The captain got George on the phone. "Dad! Is everything alright?"

"Sure son! It's it's a boy! Jennie had a boy!"

"What did she name it Dad?"

"George Arthur Watkins," replied Peter.

"That's wonderful," replied George.

So excited and relieved that they were both doing fine and he would be able to see them in a few weeks. "Dad, you're a grandpa! Wow, are you happy with that?" George asked.

"Your Mom and I are very happy George, and your Grandma Lynda is a great Grandma. She is ecstatic to be one and see her first great grandson."

"The Watkins name will live on. I can't wait to see them," shouted George.

As they hung up the phone, Peter and Cindy looked at each other, "we...we are Grandma and grandpa," and they hugged each other and laughed with joy. Hope was going to be an aunt and godmother. As she held the baby, she looked at Jennie and said, "you and my brother have a beautiful baby Jen. I suppose you are anxious to go by George."

"Oh yes Hope, I am. But when he is baptized we will send you tickets to come and be Godmother."

"Thank you Jen," said Hope. "I will be waiting. It will be an honor to be the baby's Godmother."

Hope was so excited that she forgot that she had to be at the church for the children's practice. "I have to go, Jen, I'm late for the children's choir practice." She gave Jen a hug and said, "See you tomorrow."

Jennie's Mom and Dad came into her room and told her congratulations. "Mom and Dad, what do you think of being grandparents?" Her parents face lit up like a candle.

"We are so proud to be Grandma and grandpa dear."

After Jennie and the baby were well and able to join George, everything had settled down. Peter and Cindy caught up on what was happening at the school. The staff was happy to see Peter back as he was the only one who could get through to the troubled boys. There had been a few new boys since he and Cindy had taken time out to help the Davis family get Jennie well and visit with George while on his pass home. The school meant a lot to Peter because his father George Sr. had raised him to teach others to know the love of God. He would never forget the love that George Sr. and Lynda had given him as a boy lost on the streets. So, seeing the many boys who didn't have that kind of love and no Christian schooling, he wanted to dedicate his life helping other boys. His mother, Lynda was a loving and caring Mom. She was always sure Peter and the grandchildren had the best in life that she and God could give, and now Peter and Cindy wanted to take care of her. It was their turn to let Lynda know how much she meant to them and to keep Dad and her forever in their thoughts and heart. She was the world to them, and they knew they wouldn't have her forever.

But while they still had her, they wanted to do whatever they could to make her happy and love her as much as she loved all of them, even Hope and George Jr.. Lynda knew that Hope loved her music so much, and it meant the world to her. Music was her first love but what would she do if she was alone? With George married now, and Mom and Dad getting older and Grandma not well, what would Hope do? Who would she turn to for help? She had been thinking a lot about this. She hadn't said anything to any of the family. Hope didn't want to worry them because Grandma Watkins was keeping them all busy taking care of her. She went on teaching without talking about it, but it was still on her mind. Where would George be? As the day passed, she got a call from a young man she had met in college. Hope was at work when he called and Cindy had answered the phone.

"Hello?" came the voice on the other end.

"Hello," said Cindy, "who is this that I am talking to?"

"Well, ma'am, this is a college student that knew Hope, is she there?" he asked nervously.

Cindy could sense the young man was nervous and scared.

"Sir, who are you, and may I help you?" Cindy asked.

"Well, I...I would like to see Hope if I may. She was a good friend in college, so I would like to see her if it's alright."

"Hope will be home this evening if you call

her back. Oh, may I ask you your name?"

"Sure ma'am, it's Peter. Peter Shilling. I will call her tonight."

"Wait," said Cindy, "where are you staying?"

"I'm at the hotel because I have no one here. That's why I want to see Hope's smiling face."

"Well, why don't you come over here? It's only a little way from the hotel." Cindy gave the young man the address. "I am Hope's mother."

"Alright, Mrs. Watkins, I will see you this evening, bye now."

They hung the phone up and then Cindy wondered who the young boy was and where he lived. Was he a good person for her daughter? And it struck Cindy as she said, "his name is Peter. Would we have another Peter in the family? Did Hope know him well?"

Cindy couldn't wait till Hope got home. "I better call her and let her know so she doesn't stay at work late," she thought.

Hope was finishing up practice hours and the phone rang. "Hello? Oh Hi Mom, are you okay?"

"Sure dear, but you got a phone call from a young man and he's coming over tonight to see you."

Who is it Mom?" she asked.

"Well, his name is Peter Shilling. He said he met you at college."

"Oh, Mom thanks for calling. I will be home soon, bye now." Hope was so excited that she was going to see an old friend. "I wonder if he has changed?" she said to herself. It was so exciting to her that a young man wanted to see her. "What would I say?" she asked herself. "Would he recognize me? Why is he here? I haven't seen him since we finished college, five years ago."

Hope finished her class and stopped at the store to pick out a new dress and fix her hair before she saw Peter. "Well, I better not be too excited about it." She drove home and Peter wasn't there yet, so she had time to let her Mom and Dad know a little about him. "Mom, Dad, is Peter here?"

"No, Hope, you sound so happy. Who is this young man?" asked her father.

"He is a student who studies music with me. He's very good. He helped me a lot when I ran into trouble with it. He was a very polite person," said Hope.

"We are anxious to meet this young man, Hope," they replied.

"You will like him, Dad," Hope said, "I am so surprised to hear from him."

"Well, he should be coming soon, so let's make him feel welcomed," Cindy said. "He is a stranger in town and doesn't know anyone. Does he play the piano Hope or sing?"

"He really does both, Mom. He has a beautiful voice. He lives in Atlanta where we went to college."

Hope kept pacing the floor, looking out the window, wondering when he was coming. "Come here Hope," said Peter. "He won't get here any sooner by pacing the floor."

"Dad, he is so handsome and kind. His parents had me over for meals on the weekends. I never dreamed that I would see him again. What do I say to him?"

Peter and Cindy have never seen Hope so nervous and yet so happy. Could this be a start of a new friendship for the two of them? Well, they didn't want to speculate on anything. They were also wondering what Hope would do if and when they were gone and with George so far from home. Peter, her Dad, was thinking maybe this is a sign from God that Hope will never be alone. Even so, God would take care of her and George and Jennie. They were sitting in the parlor by the fireplace and Cindy was in the kitchen fixing supper with Lynda. Lynda had been resting and Cindy helped her in her wheelchair.

"Mother," said Cindy, "we have a guest coming for supper tonight."

"Who is it?" asked Lynda.

"A young man that Hope met at College. He called this afternoon. I haven't met him yet but Hope is very excited. I hope he is a very nice person. Hope can use a friend besides the children. She doesn't get out very much and she really needs to, don't you think Mom?"

"Yes, I do," Lynda replied. "She's so busy at the school and the church. Yes, she really needs to enjoy her life a little more, with George and Jennie gone, she has been busy all the time now."

"Well, let's get supper and invite him to stay," replied Cindy.

While Hope and her Dad were enjoying each others company and waiting for her friend Peter, they were all anxious to meet the young man. Suddenly the doorbell rang and Peter answered the door where there stood a tall handsome young boy.

"Hello," said Mr. Watkins to Peter.

The young man replied. "Hello. I am Peter Schilling, Hope's friend."

"Come on in Peter," said Mr. Watkins.

As Peter entered their home, he was surprised to see how beautiful it was. "ou have a beautiful home, sir," said young Peter.

"Thank you," replied Hope's Dad and led him to the parlor room where the family was waiting for him.

"Hope! I am glad to see you! You haven't changed at all and are just as pretty as ever," said young Peter. "You do remember me, don't you?"

"Oh, yes Peter,"she replied. Hope started to introduce her Dad and Mom.

"I have met your father as I came in and briefly talked with your mother on the phone, but who is this lovely lady?"

"This is my Grandma, Lynda," replied Hope.

"Nice to meet you," and Peter shook her hand. "I came talk to you Hope, if it is okay with your folks."

"Well son," said Cindy, "we are ready to have supper, would you like to join us? After we eat supper, you and Hope can use the patio and visit."

"I would be honored to join you," replied

Peter. He joined Hope and her family at the table. Grace was said and the food was served. He and Hope would look at each other, wondering how things would go and Hope wondered what Peter had on his mind.

"Why was he here?" Hope asked herself.

"Peter, where are you from?" asked Grandma Watkins.

"I live in Alabama and went to college with Hope."

"Did you study music also?"

"Yes, I love music," replied Peter. "I play the piano just like Hope does," he said.

"And Grams," said Hope, "he has a beautiful voice, unless he lost it while I was gone, but I don't think so." (And they all chuckled).

"Peter," said Hope, "my Dad is a minister and runs the Christian school for the boys and Mom helps out. When grandpa was living, he started the school. We all miss him very much."

After the conversations were over and the table was cleared, Peter, Hope's Dad, said, "Hope why don't you and young Peter sit on the patio, you will have a little privacy there."

"Thanks Dad, we'll be outside if you need us, okay?"

Peter held the door open for Hope as they went outside. "Well, Peter Schilling what brings you here? I haven't seen or heard from you since I left Alabama."

"Well, after I finished school, I enlisted in the Navy. I was there for four years and then I was hurt on the ship and was in the infirmary for six months. Then Mom and Dad came and brought me home. I thought a lot about you Hope, but I am not a writer of words, so when I felt better, I decided to call you. I hope you don't mind," he said.

"Oh, no, I am glad that you called me, Peter. I am sorry that you were hurt, was it bad? What happened? I bet you wished that I wouldn't ask so many questions," said Hope.

"At the time that I was in the Navy, I was on tour on the coast. The troop was sent to guard the coast line but the skippers got us before we could see them. Two of the men were killed and me and Andrew got away. I was shot in the leg and Andrew carried me to safety. That's when I landed in the infirmary."

"Wow, Peter, you really had an exciting life," said Hope, "but I am glad that you are alright. What happened to your friend Andrew?"

"Well, Andrew had gone home to Germany to

see his parents."

"Germany?" asked Hope. "Why there? Aren't they the ones you were fighting against?" she asked.

"No, Hope, it was Afghanistan. Andrew was a very nice person he helped me a lot and saved my life. I owe him a lot. I hope he got home safe," Peter said. Peter was surprised at Hope's questions. "Haven't you kept up with the war over there?" he asked. "It was awful."

"Yes," said Hope, "but there's been so much going on here that I lost track of all of it the last few months. I told you that I have a brother, a twin, and his name is George, named after his grandpa who passed away a few years ago and who adopted my Dad as a young boy."

"Hope, what happened to your grandpa? Didn't you say he was the one who started the Christian school for the boys at the table?"

"Grandpa came down with bad pneumonia. We miss him and my Mom's mother also passed away. Grandma Mary was Cindy's Mom. She died shortly after Cindy and Peter were married."

"Well Hope, where is you brother?" Peter asked.

"George is in the Army overseas. He came

home on furlough because his wife was very sick and they didn't expect the baby to live, but they are all together now and doing fine. Pete, what about your Mom and Dad? I remember having dinner on the weekends. I enjoyed their company. They were so pleasant. How are they doing? Where are they?"

"Well, they are both retired now and doing some traveling that they have already been planning. They are on their way to Hawaii this week, that's why I thought I would come and see you. I'm sure glad I caught you at home Hope. Well, I guess I better let you get some of your work done but can I see you tomorrow?"

"Sure Peter, we have had a very nice evening and there's a lot more to talk about," said Hope. "I will be at the school most of the day and then I have church choir practice, but you are welcome to come and sing with us."

As they entered the house, Peter told Hope that he better be going so she can get some rest. Peter and Cindy said to Pete, "it was very nice meeting you son. Did you two have a nice visit?" Cindy asked.

Grandma said, "we hope to see you again Pete."

Peter walked him to the door and wanted

to know him a little bit better. Hope gave her parents a hug and said, "I will be back after I give Peter a ride home."

"Alright dear," they said, "drive careful and don't be gone too late."

Hope drove over to the school to show Pete where she works and gave him a tour of the building. She came to the room where she and the children practice their music daily. "Wow," said Peter and gazed at how large and beautiful the piano was.

"How about playing a duet together?"

"Alright," replied Hope, "but not too late, we might wake the boys up."

They sat down to play a soft melody so as not to wake up the boys. "Fly Away" was one of Hope's favorite songs. Then they started to sing together when one of the boys heard them and wanted a drink of water.

"Why are you up Scott?" asked Hope.

"I heard the music and it was so pretty," said Scott. "May I get a drink of water?"

"Sure, but then you crawl back in bed and I will see you tomorrow," replied Hope.

"Alright Miss Watkins and good night," said Scott.

Pete and Hope locked up and Hope took Pete home and returned home to find her Mom and Dad still waiting for her return to make sure that she was alright.

"We are glad you're home safe, Hope," they replied as they gathered around the fireplace with their Bible and called Hope to join them. "How was your visit?" they asked.

"Wonderful," replied Hope. "We caught up on a lot of memories."

"Are you going to see him again?" asked Grandma.

"Sure Grandma, he's coming to the church tomorrow while we do the choir practice."

"Where are his parents?" asked Cindy. "They are on a trip to Hawaii. They are both retired so they are doing some traveling. We talked about a lot of things but there are so many things to catch up on," said Hope.

"Sweetheart, you sound so happy and we are glad, but you need to get to know him before you get serious."

"Yes, Dad and Mom," said Hope. "He is just a friend and I will go slow. I will tell you everything in the morning."

"Alright," said Peter. They read their scripture

and called it a night.

Meanwhile, back at the hotel, young Pete didn't feel alone anymore. He hasn't been this happy for a long time. While Pete was getting ready for the night, he found himself humming and then gradually turned into singing the song that him and Hope sang together at school. Pete lay in bed thinking, "why did he wait so long to see Hope?" She had been on his mind for a long time. Maybe he would stay awhile and see if Hope would see him and maybe go steady after awhile. As Pete lay in bed, many things went through his mind and he finally fell asleep.

Hope was doing well with her diet and hadn't mentioned it to Pete yet. After going home from seeing Pete and talking to her parents, she was ready to go to bed as she was feeling weak and tired. As she went to her room, she called out, "Mom! Dad! Can you come here please?"

"Sure honey!" They could hear there was something wrong by the sound of her voice. "What's wrong, Hope?" They rushed to her side and Cindy asked, "are you okay?"

"What's wrong?" asked Peter. Maybe it was too much excitement.

"I...I don't feel so good," said Hope. "I feel very shaky and my chest hurts."

Just then, she began to feel faint. "Did you eat anything this evening?" asked Cindy.

"Yes Mom! Remember I ate supper."

Cindy and Peter were very concerned about Hope.

"My milk and medicine is in the bag in the kitchen Mom, could you get it for me please?"

"I will call the doctor," said Peter and just then Hope's Grandma Lynda came out of her room and was very worried. They all three prayed, "please, don't take her from us God. We love her Lord."

Cindy fixed Hope something to eat and let her rest until the doctor arrived and examined her.

"What is it doctor?" asked Peter.

"Her protein count is up."

"I, I'm sorry Mom and Dad to put all through this."

"Don't worry," they said. "We are your parents and we will always be here for you, no matter how old you are. Right now, we need to get you to the hospital. Your doctor will meet us there."

"Mom! Pete was going to meet me at the church for practice tomorrow. Can you call him for me? Please!"

"Yes, dear, we will call him, so don't worry okay."

Hope was very weak and sleepy. When they got to the hospital, Dr. Johnson met them in the room. "Hello," he said. "How is our patient? You gave us all quite a scare."

"She is very pale and weak doctor," said Cindy.

"Well, let's take a look." The doctor checked Hope over and replied, "we need to take some tests to see how her protein level and the liver are doing."

Hope was awake but not able to say much. "Has she had any other attacks other than this one?" asked the doctor.

"She hadn't said anything to us doctor."

"How about it Hope?" the doctor asked. "Be honest so we can help you get well."

"Only a couple of times doctor when I went off my diet," Hope replied.

"Remember when you were small and you sat on my lap and we talked about what to eat and what not to eat?" Doctor Johnson asked her.

"Yes, Doctor."

"Well, that still goes because your body can not handle protein. No meat, cheese or milk products."

"I will watch it close doctor," said Hope, "I'm sorry."

"You get some sleep Hope and I will see you in the morning," said the doctor.

"Alright doctor," said Hope. "Mom, Dad, don't forget to call Pete please."

Peter and Cindy took turns staying by her side at all times. In the morning, they needed to check in at the school and let Pete know that Hope was in the hospital and then go to the church for a board meeting. Peter stopped by the hotel to see Pete and let him know about Hope. Cindy had stayed with Hope while Peter went home to get some rest. He had things he had to do the next day, so he got home and Lynda, his Mom, was still up. "Mother, are you still up? You should be in bed."

"I was waiting for you son, to let me know how Hope is going to be. How is she?"

"She is going to be fine mother. The doctor is going to keep her for a few days," replied Peter.

Lynda wasn't able to go to the hospital as much as she wanted to.

"Where is Cindy?" she asked Peter.

"She is staying with Hope tonight. Remember mother when she was very little and we were all there for her?"

"Sure son."

"Well, that's what we are going to do now also. So, Mom let's get you ready for bed and I will take you up to see her tomorrow afternoon."

She smiled and felt better that Peter had talked to her. Now she was ready for sleep as she and Peter said their prayers together. "Good Night Mother," Peter said.

"Good Night son," said Lynda.

Peter arose the following morning and fixed Lynda breakfast and helped her with the dishes. Lynda was in a wheelchair most of the time but she was still able to stand and do a few little things by herself. "Mother, I have to do some errands this morning but I will pick you up later, will you be alright?"

"Sure son," said Lynda.

"See you later Mom," replied Peter. Peter had stopped first to pick up Pete to take a tour of the school and asked if he would like to run up to the hospital this afternoon.

"I would like that Mr. Watkins. I don't know where it is, so that would be great. How is Hope?" asked Pete. "I hope we didn't over do it last night."

"She is going through some testing this morning," said Peter. "I have a church meeting after we leave school, would you like to join me?"

"Would it be okay with the rest of the committee?" asked young Pete.

"Sure, it will give us a chance to get to know you and for you to see where Hope works with the children. Pete?" asked Peter, "what are your plans while you are here? How long do you plan on staying?"

"Well, I'm not sure. I can't afford to stay in the hotel very long. My parents will be gone for one month so I really wanted to spend time with Hope and so we can get to know each other better. She is a sweet girl and I like her very much."

"Do you have a job back home?" asked Peter.

"No sir, I just got out of the service after going to college. I studied music with Hope. I think we would make a good pair. I'm really sorry that she got sick. Is there anything that I can do for her?"

"How about a bouquet of flowers?"

"She would love that," said Peter.

"Well, here we are at the school. I guess Hope showed you some of it the other night. Did you meet any of the boys or staff?"

"No sir, they were all in bed except one boy who heard Hope and I playing and singing with

183

the music and he came out for a drink of water. He was a nice young boy and his name was Scott."

"That young lad," said Peter, "is a very musical and talented boy. He sings in the church choir."

"Why is he here?" asked Pete.

"Well, his parents are both gone and he has no relatives close by. His Dad passed away a year ago."

"Do the boys ever get to go back home?" Pete asked.

"Oh sure! They learn what it means to get along with other children and how God keeps them safe and they learn to trust in people. Many of them never were taught that there is a God who loves them. That's how I came here," said Peter.

"You! Mr. Watkins?" asked Pete.

"Yes son, mly biological parents died and I was left alone to defend for myself at the age of twelve. Lynda, who you have met and George, my father, who is gone, adopted me. It's a long story son, but someday Hope will tell you all about it. Oh, we better get to the church meeting now."

They went to the meeting and Peter introduced young Pete to the members and Pete was very comfortable with them. Then they headed to the hospital to see Hope.

"Mr. Watkins, asked Pete, may we stop and pick up some flowers for Hope?"

"I think she would like that," said Peter.

So, they stopped and picked up a dozen roses and they arrived at Hope's room and they found her bed empty and began to worry. "Nurse! Nurse! Where is my daughter? What happened?" Peter was frantic until the nurse told him that she is down having some tests.

"Would you like to wait?" asked the nurse.

"Where, where is her mother?"

"She is in the coffee shop. I will show you where it is."

"Alright," said the nurse. The nurse showed the two men where to go.

"Thank you, Nurse," they said and looked around to see Cindy having coffee and joined her.

"How is Hope?" asked young Pete.

"She is pretty weak but the doctor said that she is going to be alright," replied Cindy.

"Thank God! We were worried when we didn't see her in the room."

"They wanted to do some more tests, and they had to give her a transfusion," said Cindy, "but I am glad you are here. I need to go home and help mother get her lunch and her medications, so when Hope comes back, are you going to stay with her dear but I want to wait until she comes back to her room."

"I will come back after I take you home honey. You get some rest also."

They talked and Pete was just listening to all and wondered how he could help. Time passed and Hope had returned and they were all glad that she did because they were getting anxious to hear what was wrong. As they got back to her room, they saw a very tired girl. Peter asked her how she felt.

"I, I, I'm doing okay Dad, just tired from all the tests and I am hungry."

"I will ask the nurse if you can have something to eat," said Peter.

Cindy talked to Hope and said that she was glad she was okay, "but sweetheart, Dad and your friend will stay with you so I can go home and see Grandma. Dad will take me home and come back, alright?"

"Sure Mom, it's okay," and she looked at Pete.

"I will stay with her Mr. Watkins if it's okay with you two," replied Pete.

"Oh thank you! That's wonderful," said Mr. and Mrs. Watkins.

"I will be back later said Peter. As they left, Pete sat beside Hope's bed and had the nurse put her flowers in a vase for her.

"Thank you Pete," said Hope. They are beautiful and she smiled. "I'm glad you came. I'm sorry you had to see me like this," as she felt a little embarrassed and tears came to her eyes.

"Don't worry about it, you just get well so we can do things together. I wouldn't miss this for the world. This gives me a chance to see you, even if we didn't get to go on our date. Your Dad was very nice about picking me up. What happened Hope?" asked Pete. "Can you tell me?"

"Well, Pete, when I was born, I had a problem with protein efficiency and I have to live on a diet with no milk or meat products but I guess I went off my diet and I got real sick. Then they need to get the protein count back to normal."

"Wow!" Pete said, "I never knew there was such a thing. Are you going to be alright now?"

"I sure hope so because I'm just getting to know your family and you."

"You have very nice parents, Hope."

"Pete! Pete, how long are you staying?"

"I don't know for sure. I want to make sure that you are alright first and I need to get a job because I can't stay at the hotel as it's too expensive. I have to call Mom and see if they are back yet, but I will be here until you get better alright," said Pete.

"Thank you Pete," said Hope. She was very sleepy and Pete told her to close her eyes and that "I will be right here when you wake up."

"Your Dad will be back in a little while Hope."

She looked at Pete and said, "Pete, don't go away."

"No! Sweetheart, I'll be right here," and caressed her forehead and she slowly fell asleep. Pete never left Hope's side, but he sat and prayed that Hope would be alright and that someday, the two of them could do things together and he would always take care of her. Mr. Watkins came in to Hope's room and saw young Pete sitting next to Hope's bed praying and knew that this young boy was going to be a good friend to Hope and that maybe someday, well, his thoughts stopped and he said, "I'm back Pete. If you would like, you can go home. If Hope is sleeping, I can take you home and then come back here."

"Alright Mr. Watkins, but I can come tomorrow while you and Mrs. Watkins are at the school, if that's alright with you," said Pete.

"Sure Pete," replied Peter. "That would be very nice of you and I know that Hope will like that."

"Thank you," said young Pete. The nurse took over watching Hope while Mr. Watkins took Pete home. They were both concerned and very tired.

"Thank you again Mr. Watkins for bringing me home and for letting me stay with Hope."

"I'm glad that you and Hope got to visit a little before she got sick. It's just that she needs to be careful and eat at certain times of the day and to stay on her diet."

Peter returned to the hospital and Hope was still sleeping, so Peter curled up in a lounge chair with a book and fell asleep peacefully.

The following morning, Cindy arrived at the hospital and the doctor had come in. She and Peter were worried about Hope living alone in the house that Cindy and Peter had received for a wedding gift from his parents. Losing this house would be the last thing they wanted to happen, but Hope couldn't live alone. They didn't want to sell the house as it means too much to them. There were too many memories and they didn't want to lose them to a stranger. Their folks had furnished the house for them and it was the same now as it was back then. It has been in the family for thirty five years. They talked to the doctor and Dr. Johnson agreed that Hope could not go home alone right now as she isn't strong enough yet. They all agreed that they could not lose Hope, especially with George Jr. gone and they didn't know when he would return. They missed him, Jenny, and the baby a lot.

After the doctor came and talked to the Watkins, they returned to Hope's room. Dr. Johnson checked her over and asked how she was eating. Hope said, "I am doing a little better doctor."

"Well! Young lady, we are keeping you for another day to make sure that you are eating right. Then we will make your diet out for you but you can't live alone for awhile, okay?"

"Why doctor?" asked Hope.

"Because we need to know that you are eating right and not overdoing it, okay?"

"Yes, doctor," said Hope.

"Thank you," replied Doctor Johnson, "and I will see you tomorrow, same time and same station," as he was leaving.

Young Pete walked in and Hope's eyes opened wide as she was not expecting to see her friend again. Pete said hello to Mr. and Mrs. Watkins and walked over by Hope.

"I, I'm glad to see you feeling better," said Pete. "We sure worried about you."

Peter and Cindy asked Pete if he would mind staying with Hope so they could grab something to eat and then they had some errands to do. Thinking the two of them would have time to be alone.

"Sure, I would be glad to if it's alright with Hope, is it Hope?"

"I would like that very much," she replied. Peter was still active in the ministry, so he had things he had to see about but before he left, they said, "Hope, we will be back later to see you. Get some rest. The nurses and Pete will be here for you. Remember, God loves you and so do we!"

"I love you too Mom and Dad, bye."

Young Pete sat by her side and talked until the nurses came in and asked Hope if she would like to get up for a little while. "Oh, can I?" said Hope.

"Yes, but your friend will have to wait out in the hall if he will please."

"Sure I can do that," he said. "Let me know when it's okay. I will grab a cup of coffee and then come back."

Peter and Cindy missed George and the family and wished that they were here, but they knew he had a family of his own to care for and people who needed him as much as they do.

Peter and Cindy had stopped at the school to see how John and Jerry were doing and then they stopped at the church for a meeting where they all prayed for Hope and the family, and then headed home to be with Lynda as she was at home and they were worried about her. First they had called the hospital to check on Hope, only to hear that she was doing well and that Pete was taking her for a little walk down the hall.

"Is she strong enough to be up out of bed?" they asked.

"She is doing fine," said the nurse, "and so is her friend, he is very good to her, so there is nothing to worry about. We will see that she doesn't get too tired."

"Thank you nurse," said Peter.

"We will be back in a little while," said Cindy. "We have one more stop and then we will be there."

They had thought about the house and stopped to pick up some of Hope's things to take to their house after going to the hospital.

192

When they arrived there, Pete had gotten her back to her room and the nurse was helping her back in bed.

"Hope!" said Peter, "are you still up?"

"Yes, Dad, I had a good visit with Pete. Mom, are you going to stay?"

"Yes dear, your Dad and Pete are going to go check on your Grandma and you need to eat and get some rest."

"I am fine Mom. Pete has taken good care of me," said Hope.

"Yes, Mrs. Watkins, she has been doing very well but I do need to do a few things at the hotel."

Pete took Hope's hands and said that "I will see you tomorrow," and he walked away saying goodbye to Mrs. Watkins. Mr. Watkins also said that he walked away saying goodbye to Mrs. Watkins. Mr. Watkins also said that he would see Hope in the morning and kissed his two special gals good bye and good night.

As Peter and Pete left for home, Peter asked young Pete if he wouldn't mind helping him with a few things before I take you home. "Sure, Mr. Watkins, how can I help you?" Pete asked.

"Well, when my son George was home, he always helped me with things, I miss him being here, so, if you don't mind, I could use your help caring some things in the house," Peter said. "We are moving Hope in with us until she gets stronger. The doctor doesn't want her to live alone for awhile."

"I thought Hope was living here with you and Mrs. Watkins?" said Pete.

"No, she has her own house but stays here sometimes so she isn't alone said Mr. Watkins."

"I am glad to help you sir," replied Pete.

They carried some of Hope's clothes and music sheets into a room next to Lynda's. A quiet little place or room with bright curtains and a window to let God's light shine through.

"I'm sure she will like it here," Mr. Watkins said. When they finished, Peter Shilling said, "well, I guess I better let you take care of your mother and see that she's alright. I am glad that I could be of help."

Pete was going to walk home, but Peter Watkins said, "wait, don't go. I will check on Mother and then we can talk okay?"

"Alright," as young Peter waited in the family room, Mr. Watkins looked in on his mother who was sleeping peacefully. Then he joined young Peter where it was warm and comfortable.

"Mr. Watkins, you wanted to talk with me, is there something wrong?" asked Pete.

"Oh no, son. You have been very kind and good to our daughter and we are lucky to have met you. Hope has only mentioned you when she first moved home. We are very glad to meet you. Are your parents going to be home soon?"

"I am not sure, Mr. Watkins," replied Pete.

"Well, instead of staying at the hotel, would you like to stay at Hope's place and keep things up for her until she gets well? It won't cost you anything. You can bring her bills and mail over here and if there's anything you need, just give me a call."

"Are you sure, Mr. Watkins?"

"I am very sure Pete," replied Peter, "and you may come over here to visit anytime you would like."

"I don't know what to say, you hardly know me. I would love to," said young Peter. "Thank you."

"Okay," said Peter, "I will take you home to the hotel and you can get your things together and I will pick you up in the morning. I will give you a call before I come, okay?"

Peter drove young Pete home and returned home tired and relieved that he had chosen

Hope's friend to stay at her place while she was getting better. "He is a very nice young man," Peter thought and was glad that Hope and her friend were good for each other. As he rested a while in front of the fireplace, he read his Bible and thanked God for all of his blessings when suddenly the phone rang. Peter was startled by it and rose to answer it.

"Hello?" the line was silent for a Moment. "Hello?" said Peter again, just then the operator answered, "sir, you have a call from overseas, will you accept the call?"

"Yes, who is it?"

Just then a small voice answered. "Hello Grandpa, this is Georgie."

"George? Where is your mother?"

Little Georgie was four now and was taught how to use the phone if anything would happen. "Mommy is sick and needs help, Grandpa. Can you and Grandma come here?"

"Where is your Daddy? Georgie?"

"He, he can't come home now."

"Can Mommy talk to me, Georgie?" asked Peter.

Just then a friend took the phone and explained that Jenny was very sick and that she needed to be home with her parents and family. "Where is George?" asked Peter.

"Sir," said the voice on the phone. "This is Captain Earl Johnson. I can't reach Mrs. Watkins' parents at this time. Your grandson asked me to call you. His mother is very sick and her husband George is overseas and can't be reached."

"What is wrong?" asked Peter. "The doctors aren't sure and can't seem to help her," replied the Captain.

"How is the little boy?" asked Peter.

"He is scared and needs his family."

"Is she able to travel?" asked Peter.

"Well, only if a family member is with her," said the Captain. "She is in the hospital and little Georgie is with the neighbor. Mr. Watkins, is there any way that you could come and take her home? Or get a hold of her parents?"

"I will try calling them as they will want to know," replied Peter.

"Thank you, Mr. Watkins."

As Peter hung up the phone, his heart sank. "Oh God! What do you want me to do? How can I leave now with Hope so ill also? Should I call Cindy at the hospital?" No, he wouldn't worry her tonight but he couldn't sleep. He remembered he wrote Arthur's cell phone number down and even though it was late, he had to try to reach them as they would want to know and help their daughter. Peter got the phone and found the number.

"Where could they be?" he asked himself. He dialed the number and to his surprise, Arthur answered the phone.

"Hello!" Surprised the phone rang so late at night. "Who is calling?"

"Arthur, Arthur, this is Peter, where are you?"

"What's wrong, Peter?" asked Arthur. "Why are you calling so late? Is Jenny alright?"

"Arthur, something is wrong with your daughter. The Captain called and said that Jenny is in the hospital and needs her family."

"Peter, where is she? I haven't heard from her for a while. We are worried about them," said Arthur. "Do you have the number?" Peter gave Arthur the phone number and knew that they would call their daughter, rather than the captain. He was glad he had reached her Dad because he was worried about Hope and didn't want to leave his mother alone at night, but where was his son George? Why hasn't he heard from him? No letter or any word from him for quite some time now. Peter would pray about it and wait for

God's answer. He sat for a long time and then he heard his mother's voice call out.

"Son! Why are you still up? It is quite late. What is wrong? You never sit up this late."

Lynda was very concerned about her son. "Mother, I am sorry I woke you up. I am fine, please go back to bed. Come, I'll help you. I am very tired and ready for bed also."

Peter helped Lynda back to bed and went to his room but could not sleep. "God! If you are listening, I need our answer to let me know that my son George is alright. His wife and son need him, Please! Send me a sign or something. I don't ever doubt your love." As Peter left the prayer in God's hands, he finally fell asleep.

At the hotel, young Pete couldn't sleep either. He was excited about moving into a house that Hope's parents received for their wedding and it is still in the family. He thought about his Mom and Dad and when would they be home. He missed them and wanted to tell them all the news.

As Peter finished his errands, he wondered about his grandson's phone call last night and thought he would call the Captain to see how little Georgie was and if the Davis's had gotten a hold of them. As he dialed the number, he waited till the Captain answered.

"Hello?" the Captain said.

"Captain, this is Peter Watkins. My grandson Georgie called last night, did you get a hold of Jenny's parents?"

"Yes, Mr. Watkins, they called last night. Thank you for your help. I will meet them at the airport in the afternoon. Your grandson is alright Mr. Watkins. He just misses his Mom and Dad."

"We miss them also," replied Peter. "Can you tell me anything about where my son George is?"

"I'm sorry sir, I can't say, but I can tell you that he is fine and wished he could be with his family. It is the army regulations."

"I understand, Captain, thank you. Would you have the Davis family call us when they arrive there?"

"Yes, sir, I sure will," said the Captain.

After the call to the Captain, Peter was a little more satisfied and glad that the Davis's had made arrangements to bring Jenny home. As he was on the phone to Cindy, he looked up at the sky and said, "Thank you, Lord." He picked up Pete and dropped his things off at Hope's place and then went to the hospital, knowing his wife Cindy would be very tired and ready to go home.

When he arrived, Cindy and Hope were sitting in the coffee shop. "Well, look at you, my young ladies. It is so good to see you up and looking so cheerful," and he gave each one of them a hug. "Hope, do you remember this young fellow?" asked Peter.

"Dad! Of course I do," as she smiled at Pete and he gave her a big hug.

"Well, while you are recovering by our house, Pete is going to stay by your house instead of the hotel."

"That's great, Dad," said Hope and Cindy.

"Have you seen the doctor today?" asked Peter.

"Yes, Dad, I can go home tomorrow and he said that I am doing fine."

"Well, I am bringing Grandma Lynda up this afternoon. She is anxious to see you. So, I am going to take your mother home so she can get some rest. Pete? Would you want to stay and visit with Hope?" asked Peter.

"I would love that, Mr. Watkins."

"Alright, Cindy and I will see you later when I bring Grandma up to see you. So, you take care and get some rest." They hugged her and said goodbye.

"She will be fine," said Pete.

"Thank you, Pete,' said Peter as they left to go take care of Lynda, who was anxiously waiting for Peter to come home. As they drove home together, in silence, Cindy could tell that there was something on Peter's mind and asked him, "Peter dear, did something happen at home? You are being very quiet today."

"Well, yes dear," he replied.

"What's wrong?" she asked.

"Our grandson called me last night. He was very scared and he was crying. I was just going to bed when he called and it was quite late."

"Well, what was wrong?" asked Cindy. "Where was Jenny?"

"Jenny is very sick, dear. She is in the hospital and Georgie is staying with a neighbor. The Captain took the phone from little Georgie and wanted to know if we could come and get them as they can't come home alone."

"Oh Peter! What are we going to do?" asked Cindy. "That little boy must be awful lonesome but…but…where is George?"

"George is overseas and the Captain couldn't

tell us where he is, but I gave him my word that I would call Arthur and Anna. Then they could take care of the family. I was very worried about little George as his is only three years old."

"You did the right thing dear, I am sorry that you are going through so much right now, but you know, God doesn't give us any more than we can handle and Hope will be coming home tomorrow. Everything will work out alright."

As they arrived home to pick up Lynda, she was excited about going to lunch with Peter and Cindy. Peter helped Cindy inside with some of Hope's things and gave her Mom a big hug. "Are you alright, Mom?" she asked.

"Oh sure, sweetheart. I am anxious to see our granddaughter. How is she?"

"Well, you will soon see for yourself mother," said Peter as he helped her in the wheelchair. "We are going for lunch and then up to see Hope."

Lynda smiled and said, "I can't wait to see her son."

Cindy was too tired and said that she would like to rest for a while if they didn't mind.

"That's alright, dear," Peter said. "Mom and I will be fine, won't we Mom?"

"Sure we will," said Lynda. "You get some rest."

Peter and Lynda left to go to their favorite restaurant by the boys school and then went to see Hope and Pete. As they got to Hope's room, Pete was curled up in the chair next to Hope and she was sleeping peacefully, so they were very quiet trying not to awake them. The whole family and Pete had a very busy week but now things were getting better except with the new problem and they hadn't told Hope about. They would wait till she got home and a little stronger. Then Peter nudged young Pete on the shoulder so as not to wake up Hope. Pete was a little startled and sat up and said hello to Lynda as she asked Pete, "how is she doing?"

"She is going home tomorrow the doctor said," replied Pete.

"That's great news," said Lynda. "You have been wonderful by helping her and I suppose you got the beautiful flowers also?"

"Yes ma'am, but it was your son's idea. I am glad that I could help out."

"You have done more than we could ask of you. Thank you Pete," Lynda said.

Hope finally woke up and they visited for some time until her Grandma whom she was so surprised to see got very tired. "Well, Hope, I think we will let you rest and have your meal. The nurse will be here if you need her, okay?"

"Sure Dad, I will be fine. Are you going to give Pete a ride home?" Hope asked.

"Sure, Pete, are you ready to go home?"

"Yes sir," he replied.

"Hope, are you going to be alright?"

"Sure, you go get some rest and I will see you tomorrow."

They all said goodbye to Hope and took Lynda home and Pete went to his new living quarters. "Thank you Mr. Watkins for letting me stay here. I will be glad to help wherever I am needed. Thank you again and goodnight."

As the days went on with no word from the Davis's, Peter and Cindy called them to find out what they could do to help them. Arthur and Anna were glad that they called because they had gotten to their daughter and were glad to see their grandson Georgie.

"Arthur, how are things going with Jenny and Georgie?"

"We are bringing them home in a day or so. We need to fill out some papers for release of the hospital."

"Does Jenny know where George is?" Peter asked.

"We don't know because she is not able to talk. We don't know what is wrong with her. The doctors are puzzled."

"Some blood disease? Can we do anything to help you?" Peter asked.

"Peter, do you think that Cindy and you could keep Georgie for a while?"

"Sure, we would be happy to keep him till you're ready too. We know how it is. Hope is doing okay and she is coming home from the hospital tomorrow."

"Oh Peter," said Anna, "I, we didn't know, is she okay?"

"She is much better and will be fine. We will keep everyone in our prayers at church on Sunday."

The days passed and the Davis's had Jenny and Georgie home. Jenny was in the hospital and Georgie stayed at Cindy and Peter's. Grandma Lynda loved having little Georgie with them. She has her great grandson now and was happy. Pete had not heard from his parents for a few days. He thought he would call them in the morning. He got his things ready to move into Hope's house in the morning and then would call his parents. In the morning, Pete rose early with the sun shining in the window, picked up the phone and called his parents.

"Hello!" Pete heard. It was so good to hear their voice.

"Mom! This is Pete. How are you and Dad? I haven't heard from you lately. I have missed you."

"We are fine, Pete, how are you?"

"I am okay, Mom. Are you back from Hawaii?"

"Yes, son, we got back yesterday. It was a very nice trip but we are glad to be home. Where are you, Pete?"

"I am in Rome, Georgia. How is Dad?"

"He's fine. He is resting from the long trip. What are you doing there?" she asked.

"I came to see an old friend from school and I am staying at her house until she gets better."

The day was a busy one for young Pete and Peter. Peter fixed little Georgie's and Lynda's breakfast and Cindy helped get them up and ready for the day. "I must go darling, if you need me or anything, give me a call, okay?"

Peter drove over to Hope's house and picked up Pete to go by the school to see John and Jerry. When he picked up young Pete, they were both quiet and then Peter said, "Pete, would you like to go to the school with me first? I need to stop by and see how things are."

"I would love to Mr. Watkins. Hope showed me some of it the first night I came here."

He was anxious to meet the children and the pastor and staff.

"I think you will like the boys. They are very polite, that is most of them are. Sometimes we get a lad that has had trouble at home and is not disciplined," Peter said.

"First, I need to call the hospital to see what time Hope can be released," Peter said. When Peter called Hope's room, Hope answered, "Hi Dad. Are you okay?"

"Hope? Can you come home?"

"I'm fine, and yes, I can, but I need to wait for the doctor to sign the papers and talk to me about my diet."

"Okay, sweetheart, I will be there after I stop at the church and the school. Pete is coming with me."

"Alright Dad, tell Pete that I miss him and I love you Dad, bye."

Peter and Pete continued their way to the school first. Peter had become quite fond of Pete and hoped that he would want to work at the school with Hope. He doesn't have a job and didn't know anyone, so this would be a good way for him to meet other people. As they arrived at the school, the boys were glad to see him and yelled out, "Peter! Peter!"

"Hi boys," said Peter. "How are you all?"

"Fine Peter, are you going to stay? How is Hope?"

"Well, not all day because I need to go and bring Hope home from the hospital."

They were wondering when she was coming back.

"Peter! We don't have a music teacher."

"Boys, I want you to meet a very dear friend of Hope's. Can you welcome Pete Shilling?"

The staff also joined them and they all together said, "Hello, Mr. Shilling, welcome to our school."

"Thank you boys," said young Pete.

Peter continued to show Pete the rest of the school and the staff members. When Peter introduced Pete as a music teacher and went to school with Hope, the staff was happy to meet someone who enjoyed music as much as Hope.

"Well, maybe we could hire you to take Hope's place until she comes back", said Mr. Olson, the pastor.

Pete looked at Peter and said, "Well, what do you think Peter?"

"I don't want to replace Hope."

"Well son, you could always do it while Hope is getting stronger and we could always use an extra hand around here. Isn't that right, Mr. Olson?"

"It sure is, we could use your help with so many boys."

"Well, sure, I would love to."

Pete knew he found a place where he felt needed and could help. Thank you so very much sir. They shook hands and Peter and his new friend Pete continued to head for the church after taking Pete's things to the house. Pete had already met some of the staff members and felt comfortable seeing them.

The following day, Peter and Cindy went to pick up Hope from the hospital and then would explain to her what was going on with Jenny. How would she take it? They would wait until she got settled at home. Hope hasn't mentioned them since her friend Pete came into her life. She would be surprised to see her nephew at home. When they got to the hospital, Hope was dressed and waiting for them. She was excited to go home. "Hi darling," Cindy said and hugged her. "Are you ready to go home?"

"Sure, Mom, where is Pete?" asked Hope.

"Well, he had some things to do so he couldn't make it, but he will be over at the house later, dear."

"Okay Dad, I am ready to go."

The nurse came in with a wheelchair to take her to the car as Peter and Cindy carried her things and Pete's flowers.

As they reached home, Hope was so surprised to see little Georgie there. "Mom, how did little Georgie get here? Are Jenny and George here?"

"No dear," said Peter. "We will explain when you get settled in, okay?"

"Okay Dad," so excited. "He has grown! He is so big! Where's Jenny?"

"You have to calm down, Hope."

He took her to her room where she saw pictures of God and was tired. So they left her to rest for a while.

Young Pete was getting things settled at the house and then was going to see Hope in the evening. He had to call his parents and let them know about his new job and about Hope. He was making a whole new life for himself. He never dreamed that he would be welcomed by Hope's Mom and Dad. They had made me feel so welcomed and part of the family and his parents were happy for him and had planned on meeting them soon when they would visit Pete. Things had finally settled down at the Watkins home. Hope was doing better and little Georgie was sharing a room with Grandma Watkins. He missed his Mom very much. Peter and Cindy had their hands full but loved having their family home. Pete had stopped over every day to see Hope. The two of them talked about school, work, and things that they both shared together. As weeks passed, Hope recovered and went back to work with Pete and the boys. She and Pete worked together at the school and the church.

Jenny was struggling with her illness. They had taken all sorts of test and x-rays but for some reason, she slipped into a coma. Peter and Cindy helped Arthur and Anna as much as they could. Anna asked Cindy, "is there any way we can get a hold of George?"

"There's got to be a way," said Arthur.

"We will call Washington in the morning and see if we can get a hold of him," said Peter.

"She needs him. Maybe if she hears little

Georgie's voice that will help. It's worth a try," said Arthur.

"We will bring him to see her tomorrow," replied Cindy.

They gathered to say a prayer over Jenny and Cindy and Peter left to see how Hope and Pete were doing. To their surprise, the two of them and the boys were all singing Peter's favorite song, "How Great Thou Art."

"You two are going to make a great team, it sounded wonderful," said Peter.

"Thanks, Dad," replied Hope and Pete.

"It's one of your favorite songs."

"Yes, it is," Peter replied. "Well, I am heading home to see how my grandson is doing."

"Dad, how is Jenny? Can we help in any way?"

"Just pray for her, as she has gone into a coma," said Peter.

"May we stop by and see her later?"

"Sure, Anna would like that."

Peter left for home to see little George. His thoughts were on his son George. Someone has to know where he is. They need to tell us where he is. George had been hurt once before so that bothered Peter. "Where could he be?" he asked himself. I have got to find him. He was worried that Jenny might not make it this time. He arrived at home where his wife and family were waiting. Peter picked up little Georgie and hugged him.

"You look just like your Daddy," he said.

Hope and Peter had come for supper and the family gathered at the table and thanked God for all their blessings, and asked God to help them find George. Peter was very worried, why have these things happened, first Hope and now Jenny and not knowing where his son is. Peter knew there had to be a reason but what? Is there one thing he is supposed to do for God, but what? As the evening passed, young Pete went home and the rest of the family prayed before going to bed. Maybe tomorrow will be better, he thought and said goodnight to little George and Hope and Lynda.

In the morning, as the sun rose bright and beautiful, they looked out the window and said, "dear God, thank you for your light and a new day."

Little George came running to his grandpa Peter, and Peter gathered him in his arms. "You know what, Georgie?"

"No, Grandpa, what?"

"We are going to fly to Washington."

"Why, Grandpa?"

"So we can get a hold of your Daddy. Washington must know where he is."

"I hope so, Grandpa. Is Grandma coming also?" asked Georgie as he pointed to Cindy.

"No son, Grandma has to stay with great Grandma Lynda, okay?" said Peter.

"I hope we can find Daddy. Mommy needs him, she is really sick."

Peter and little Georgie took the first flight out in the morning, anxious to find his son. "Where could he be?"

Little did they know, Jenny passed away during the night. Anna had called Cindy right after Peter and Georgie had left. "Oh no!" said Cindy. "Peter has just left to find George."

"Where did he go?" asked Anna.

"He and Georgie went to Washington. Anna, what can I do? I will call Hope and she can come over by Lynda and I will come to your house. I am so sorry!"

Anna and Arthur were in tears. They had lost their only child. Was this in God's plan, she had wondered. What will George do? Cindy was also in tears, not knowing what to tell little Georgie and what will George do. Cindy comforted Anna and Arthur. Anna and Arthur knew it was going to be hard on their grandson and George. "Cindy, what are we going to tell the family? The Army must have kept him informed," said Arthur.

"I don't know," she said.

"We need to get a hold of Peter and let him know so the Army can send George home."

Cindy left Anna and Arthur to talk to God while she made some phone calls. First she called her husband Peter who was on his way to Washington.

Peter was almost there when the phone rang. He answered with a scratchy hello.

"Peter, this is Cindy, where are you?"

"I am almost to Washington. Are you alright?"

"Yes, dear," she said with a sobbing voice. "Peter! I need to tell you something."

"What Cindy?" Peter asked. "What's wrong?"

"Peter, Jenny," she paused, "Jenny died during the night."

"Oh no, Cindy! How are the Davis's? I, I'm so sorry. I won't tell little Georgie until we get home. We need George to come home. He has got to be alright Cindy," said Peter.

"How is Hope? She is fine darling. Pete is taking good care of her. I need her to come and stay with

Lynda. I am staying with Anna and Art. Peter, please call as soon as you find George, alright?"

"Sure dear, ask Pete to keep the music going at the school okay. Cindy? I will see you as soon as we get a hold of our son. Yes dear, hurry home, I miss you."

As Peter arrived at the airport, he and little George took a cab to the Army base to see what they could do.

As they reached the base, they saw the General sitting at a desk and stopped and asked General Bird if he and little Georgie could talk to him. "Sure! Come on in. How may I help you and this little one?"

"Sir," said Peter, "we need to find this little boy's father. His name is George Watkins, my son."

"What is your name?" the general asked.

"I am Peter, his father and this is his son. My name is Peter Watkins."

"Well, we can't give information out that is special assignment duties, but we need to know the reason for this visit," said General Bird.

"Well, may I talk to you in private?"

He sat little Georgie on a chair and walked over by the general. "Sir, the boy doesn't know yet, but his mother passed away last night and her husband, my son George, needs to know and come home." Peter being a pastor restrained himself from tears which the general could see.

"I'm very sorry Mr. Watkins," the general replied. "Have a seat and I will see what we can do for you."

He pulled out George's records and looked through them. "When was the last time that you heard from your son?"

"It's been a long time, sir. We have tried many times but we couldn't get him to answer our calls. I hope that you can help us, General."

"Let me see what I can do, Peter." He got on the phone to the major and heard George was shipped back to the states last week. "I can give you the base that he would be on," said the major. "Thank you," replied the General.

Returning to his office, he told Peter that George was shipped back to Cherry Point in North Carolina for the rest of his term. "I can call them and have them contact you right away, sir."

"Thank you, General Bird," said Peter. "I am very grateful for your help. His wife was very sick and he doesn't know that she passed away yet. I know it will be a shock to him."

"Well, as soon as he gets the message, I'm

sure he will call. He will be able to get a funeral leave. You may wait here in town close by and he will call you soon, sir," said the General.

"Thank you, General," Peter said and Peter picked up little Georgie and waited at a restaurant close by.

Back home, Cindy had called Hope and Pete. Hope was very upset and cried hard. "Pete," she said, "I need to go home and stay with Grandma."

She couldn't hold the tears back. Pete took her in his arms and asked what had happened. "My sister-in-law, Jenny, passed away last night." Holding the tears back, she said Pete, "can you stay with the boys."

"Sure, sweetheart."

He had never called her that before. It felt so wonderful. "Thank you Pete," said Hope. She told the boys that she had to leave, but Pete would help them with the music. Pete was happy to do it but was worried about Hope. Hope arrived at home by Lynda who asked her if she was okay. "I'm okay, Grams. How are you?"

"I'm a little hungry," she said not knowing what had happened to Jenny. "I will fix you some breakfast. What would you like, Grams?" asked Hope. Grandma just wanted a piece of toast and some oatmeal. Then she asked, "where is everyone, Hope?"

"Grams, I guess Mom is over by Arthur's and Anna's and Dad is with little Georgie."

She didn't want to upset her grandmother. She fixed her breakfast and helped Lynda get dressed. "Where did Peter and Georgie go?" Lynda asked Hope.

"Well, Grams, I might as well tell you but promise me that you won't get upset okay."

"Sure dear, you can tell me."

"Grandma, did Mom tell you about Jenny? She did say that Jenny was very ill, how is she now?"

"Grandma, Jenny passed away last night."

"Oh no! Hope! What was wrong with her, Hope?"

"They don't know, they took all types of tests and didn't find anything. I will really miss her," said Hope.

"So will we all dear," said Lynda. "Hope, where is George? Does he know?" asked Lynda.

"Dad and little Georgie flew to Washington to get some answers to the whereabouts of George. He hasn't called back yet but he will."

"Hope, how is Anna and Mr. Davis? It must be very hard on them. Jenny was their only child."

"I'm sure it is Grams, but Mom is there to help them."

As the day went on, Hope was waiting to hear from Peter about George and young Pete had finished the day at the school and had stopped over to help Hope. As the evening had gone slow, they sat and hoped to hear from Peter when suddenly the phone rang. "Hello?" said Hope.

"Hello Hope, are you alright?" asked Peter.

"Dad! Where are you? Are you on your way home?"

"I am okay and little Georgie and I will be home tomorrow. Is Mom there?"

"No Dad, did you find George? Is he coming home?" asked Hope.

"Yes, Hope, the General Bird called the major and he got the information to George. He will be meeting us tomorrow and we will all fly home together. Please let your mother know, alright?"

"Sure Dad! Thank God that he's alright," said Hope.

"Yes dear, thank God for that. Well, we will see you all tomorrow."

Hope hung up the phone all excited and yet in tears that they were all going to be home. Dad found George and they are all coming home tomorrow. "Oh Pete, I can't wait to see George. He has been gone for a long time." He took Hope in his arms and held her close. "Pete, you will like my brother, he's very kind. He's a pastor just like my Dad."

They talked a while and Hope helped Lynda to bed while Hope and Pete visited with her for a while and then Pete said he better get going. "Pete! Can you handle the boys tomorrow? They seem to like you."

"Yes Hope, for you anything. The boys will be fine. I'm sure that John and Jerry will help with them. So you get some rest okay, and I will see you tomorrow."

Pete kissed Hope goodbye and she left to finish her work and then she called Cindy. Cindy was still up with the Davis's and the family when the phone rang. "Hi Hope," she said, "are you okay?"

"Yes Mom, how are you? Grandma is in bed."

"I'm very tired but Anna needs someone so I will stay tonight."

"Mom! Dad called. He will be home tomorrow."

"Did they find George?"

"Yes, they did, Mom. George will come home tomorrow with them."

Cindy's voice sounded happy but couldn't help but cry. "Mom! It's going to be okay. Please, tell Anna and Arthur that it is going to be okay and I will see you tomorrow."

"Okay dear," replied Cindy, "goodnight."

Cindy told the Davis's that Peter had reached George and that they would all be home tomorrow. Anna and Arthur were relieved and shed tears together with Cindy.

"Well," said Cindy, "let's all pray for their safety home and get some rest."

She waited until Anna and Arthur were settled down and she curled up in a lounge chair where she fell asleep the rest of the night.

The following day was a trying day for all of them. George was coming home. Where has he been? How would he feel? What would he do without Jenny. They had gotten home in the early afternoon. Anna and her husband and Cindy all welcomed them home with open arms. George tried to hold back his tears but when he saw Anna, he broke down and cried. "Anna, I am so sorry. I didn't know. No one told me that she was so ill. I really miss her."

"It's alright, son," Anna replied in tears, "it's not your fault. How are you, George?"

"Mom, Dad, I need to see you! Please!"

Peter took George's hand and said, "son." He hadn't told George that Jenny was gone. "George! I need to tell you that Jenny is gone. I'm sorry, son."

"NO! Dad, what happened?" asked George. "Anna, where is she? I want to see her."

"Peter, do you and Cindy mind if Arthur and I talk to George? He needs to see her okay. We will talk later."

The Davis's and George went to their house and took George to see his Jenny. "Why? Why did God take her? Why?" He couldn't understand it. He couldn't believe that this happened to him after helping many of the soldiers that were dying but couldn't help his own wife get well. "What did I do wrong?" he thought. After he and the Davis's saw Jenny, they went home where George saw pictures of Jenny and Georgie. "If only I hadn't joined the Army," he said to Arthur. "Maybe this wouldn't have happened."

"George," said Arthur, "we are so sorry. She was our only child. We will miss her, but you need to think about little Georgie. Does he know?"

"No, he knows that she was awfully sick. I don't know what to tell him."

"Well, son, we will cross that bridge tomorrow alright?"

George wiped his eyes and looked at them, "you two have really lost your daughter. She meant the world to you, didn't she?"

"Yes, she did, son, but I guess God needed her more than he thought we did, so let's remember her through her son and you, alright?"

"Thank you for your help. Now I must let you get some rest. You must have had a hard time."

George and the family said goodbye to Jenny and welcomed friends and neighbors to say their goodbyes also. The service was beautiful.

Weeks passed after George took care of everything with Jenny's family and told little Georgie about his Mom. He wasn't ready to go back to finish his time, but he knew he had to. It wouldn't be easy. Little Georgie would stay with his grandpa and Grandma. George said goodbye to Peter and Cindy and said that he would return in two months. Then he was done in the Army. He missed his family a lot and hated to leave.

Young Pete and Hope would miss him also. Pete and George had become friends. Pete and Hope worked well together and became very close. One day after all troubles calmed down, he asked Peter and Cindy if they would mind if he asked Hope to marry him. Hope didn't know that he had asked her parents. "Pete, will you say that again?" they said, shocked but yet amazed.

"Well, Mr. and Mrs. Watkins, I want to ask Hope to marry me, if that is alright with you folks?"

Peter shook hands with Pete and Cindy hugged him, "but I think we all better ask Lynda just to see her expression."

"You mean? Really?" Pete was very excited as they joined Lynda in the parlor room.

"Mom! Pete has something to ask you."

"Grandma Lynda, would you mind if I marry your granddaughter?"

Lynda looked at Pete and said, "I think you will make Hope very happy," and she smiled. He gave her a hug and said, "thank you all. Now, I can pop the question when Hope gets home," but Pete couldn't wait. When Hope arrived home, everyone was quiet and ready for supper.

"Come on Hope," called her Grandma.

"I'm coming, Grams," as they all chucked quietly.

"Well, Pete, would you mind saying grace tonight?" asked Peter. Hope looked at Pete and then at the rest of the family wondering why her Dad had asked Pete to say grace.

"I would be honored to."

As Pete said thanks to God and the family, he reached into his pocket and turned to Hope who was sitting next to him and he took her hand and said: "Hope, will you marry me?"

She smiled, thinking that he was joking. So, he said it again, "will you marry me, Hope?" Hope looked at her Dad and Mom, "well," Peter said, "what is your answer?"

"I, I'm surprised and yes, I will marry you," replied Hope...and Pete kissed her and placed the ring on her finger as everyone clapped their hands and said congratulations, then they finished their meal.

"We are glad to welcome you to our family Pete, George will be glad also."

"We worry about George, I hope he is alright," said Hope. "Maybe he can stand up for our wedding?"

"Hope, don't make it too soon. It might not be too good for George. It will bring up too many memories for him," replied Cindy.

"We won't, Mom," Hope said and looked at Pete and smiled.

"No ma'am, there are many things that we need to do, and we do want George to feel better," replied Pete. "We want him to be a part of our wedding and also little Georgie."

"We will help the two of you all we can," Lynda said.

"I am looking forward to it. Dad," said Hope, "do you think that Pete and I can live in the house that you and Mom got for your wedding? Do you think that George and little George will mind?"

"I, I will have to talk to George when he comes home," Peter replied. Jenny and George were to move in there when he was released from the Army and Peter couldn't promise it to Hope until he talked to George.

Anna and Arthur had joined the Watkins for supper the night George went back to the service. When Hope asked about the house, Anna and Arthur thought for a Moment.

"Peter, Cindy, when Georgie and his Dad are together again, would you mind if they stayed with us until George is ready to be himself again? It would be company for us and we would love to have Jenny's son, our only grandson living with us. It is going to be lonesome for all of us."

"I'm sure that would be alright with us,"

replied Peter, "but let's not talk about it until George gets home. Hope and Pete don't want to rush the wedding and they want George to be comfortable with it."

"Alright Peter," said Anna. "Well, Cindy and Hope, it was a good evening and I know that things will be alright. Thank you for your dinner and company this evening. We will be leaving now," said Anna and Arthur. "May God be with you all," Anna said.

"Bye Anna and Arthur and please call us if you need anything," said Peter.

"Yes Peter, we will and again, thank you."

As Anna and Arthur returned home, they went to Jennifer's room, "look dear," said Anna, "we will never see our daughter again," tears flowing from her eyes.

"Come dear," Arthur said, "let's go to bed. She will always be here and our grandson will keep her alive."

"Yes darling, Georgie will be a lot of Jenny. He will miss his mother very much so, let's go to bed and worry about that when they come home."

They worked all month preparing the house for George and their grandson. It would help them to get over Jenny's death and keep their mind on her son. As the months passed, the Watkins and the Davis' patiently waited to hear from George. He was to come home soon and they couldn't wait, and Hope couldn't wait to tell him about them getting married. Would he be happy for her? They were all anxious to see him.

Peter and Cindy had kept little George till he came home, then it was up to George to take care of his son. George's time was up and he got his dismissal from the Army. He called his Dad to meet him at the airport. "Dad! Will you pick me up at the airport tomorrow?"

He wasn't ready to see everyone yet. "Sure I will, son, do you want mother to come?" asked Peter.

"No, Dad, please come alone. I want to talk to you alone, okay?"

"Sure son, I will be there, what time George?" asked Peter.

"My plane will be there at 4:30."

"Alright George," Peter said, "I will see you then son and I love you, bye." Peter didn't say anything to the family but prayed that night that everything would be okay.

Hope and Cindy knew it was close to the time that George should be home but wasn't sure when. She and young Pete worked well as a team. Peter wondered why George didn't want his mother to come with him to pick him up at the airport. He knew that George had gone through a lot but what did he want to talk to him about? He was hoping it was good news. Maybe it was just a little time alone before he saw everyone.

Peter met George at the airport the next day and thought to himself how nice and handsome George looked in his Army uniform. George walked up to his Dad and they smiled and embraced each other. "You look wonderful George," said Peter.

"Thank you Dad, I feel great but I still miss coming home to Jenny. But I know that she is in good hands with God, although I couldn't believe that he would take her away from little Georgie and I, but when I got back to the base, my crew greeted me there and it made me feel better."

As they drove to a restaurant to talk, they were both quiet and ordered some coffee while waiting for their food. Soon George broke the silence. "Dad, I am glad that we are alone. How is little Georgie?" he asked.

"He is just fine, George. He still asks for his Mommy, but we tell him that God called her home because he needed her to help him in heaven."

"Dad! What am I going to do?"

"What do you mean son?" asked Peter.

"Well, I have signed up for four more years."

"What! Why George?" asked his Dad, "why would you do that? What about your son?" Peter was shocked and didn't know what to say. "George, is this, what you really want?"

"Yes Dad, it is. I have seen so many soldiers lost and alone and I feel that I can be there to help them."

"What about little Georgie?" Peter asked.

"Dad, I want my son to be with me. I need him with me and we will be fine."

Peter didn't know what to say. "Dad, you always said that God chooses us for his work no matter where we go right? Wherever he sends us, we must follow, right Dad?"

"What about little George?" asked Peter.

"He will go to a good school and I will be home in the evenings," said George. "He will grow up to be a Christian, Dad."

"I am really happy for you if that's what you want, but I don't know how your mother will take it," said Peter.

"Oh! George," said Peter as they ate their meal.

"Yes, Dad, what?"

"Hope and Pete are getting married, so we hoped that you can come home for the wedding."

"Wow!" said George, "when is the big day?" he asked.

"Well, they haven't set a date yet because they want you to stand up for them, but they didn't want to make it too soon after Jenny's death seeing what you went through. George I know Anna and Arthur asked if you and your son could stay by them. It would make them feel like they have a family again."

"I, I don't know how to tell them about going back into the service, Dad."

"Well, they will be fine, George. You need to tell them though, okay? I will be glad to go with you son."

"Thank you, Dad, I know that this is what God chose for me. I, I can't believe that my twin sister is getting married. Pete is a very nice person and I hope that they will be happy, Dad. I will be here for the special day even if I have to take off from the Army at that time."

"Hope will be glad to hear that. She wouldn't get married without her twin brother," said Peter.

Cindy and Hope were wondering where Peter

went because he hadn't said anything to them about meeting George.

When Peter and George had discussed all their business, they headed for home. When they walked into the door, Cindy was so surprised that she cried and gave George a hug.

"Why didn't you let us know that you were coming home?" said Cindy.

"Mom! Come here."

"I'm coming Cindy, what is it?" Lynda was slow at getting there so Cindy went and helped her, but she didn't tell her what it was that she wanted. Lynda was so surprised.

"George! How are you? I am happy to know that you are home and alright."

George gave Grandma a big hug. "I love you Grandma," said George. They talked all hours of the night, but George peeked in at his son who was sleeping peacefully so he didn't disturb him.

"Dad, do you think that Arthur and Anna would be sleeping?" asked George. "Will it be too late to call them?"

"I am sure that they will still be up, son. They haven't slept too good lately since Jenny passed away. I think it might help them to hear from you, son," replied Peter.

George gave the Davis's a call.

"Hello?" said Arthur.

"Hi Mr. Davis, this is George."

"George! Where are you? It's so good to hear your voice."

"I am at Dad's. I got in late this afternoon. Arthur, are you and Anna going to be home tomorrow?" asked George.

"Yes, George, are you coming over?"

"Little Georgie and I will be over in the morning, if it's alright with you and Anna?"

"Of course it is, George. We always want to see you and our grandson," said Anna.

As he finished talking, Cindy said, "George we don't have any pictures of you in your uniform. Can we get one of all of us together and one of you and little Georgie in the morning? We have a camera that we can set up and get all of us on camera together."

"Sure, Mom," said George.

Young Pete was there also with Hope and he was going to take the picture but George said, "Pete, you and Hope get in here also."

George knew that Pete would be part of the family also when Hope and him got married. "I hear you will be part of our family soon."

Hope looked at Dad and smiled. "Alright," said Pete and after the family picture, they took one of the five of them as a family picture. George looked so great in his uniform. "Well, I guess we better let Grandma get some rest and you also Hope. I hear that you have been quite ill, but I am glad that you're okay now," said George.

"I am doing great George. The family has been wonderful and so has Pete. Good to see you, bro!"

Hope and Lynda retired for the night while George and his parents sat in the living room. George had to tell his Mom what his plans were for the future. As they gathered in the family room, Cindy said to George, "son, what are your plans now since you are out of the service?"

Peter and George looked at each other, not sure how to tell his Mom that he was rejoining or enlisting for a second term. George looked at his Mom and said, "Mom, I might as well tell you now. Dad and I talked a lot about this this afternoon when I got off the plane. There are so many children and lost people who are starving and need clothes and shelter and medicine."

"I'm sure there are many who do," Cindy replied.

"Many need love and don't know who God is. I can help the ones who are hurt."

"So, what does this have to do with the future George?" Cindy asked.

Cindy said, "Peter, George is trying to tell you that he enlisted for four more years. He feels that this is God's calling."

"Yes, Mom, there is so much to do," replied George.

"George, what about Hope and Pete's wedding? Are you going to be here?"

"Mom, I wouldn't miss her big day for anything. I am going to be the best man. I hope you aren't too disappointed, Mom. This is what I want to do."

"George?" asked Cindy, with tears in her eyes, "what about your son?"

"Mom, little Georgie is going with me. They have wonderful schools and he will get good care. I want to see my son grow up and not see him every few months." George realized that he was upsetting his Mom. "Mom!" He put his arms around her and said, "it is going to be alright. I'm not in the war zone area so it will be alright for little George to go with me. He will be with other children."

"When do you need to go back?" asked Peter.

"I am on leave for four months, so I can spend some time with the boys and Anna and Arthur. When is Hope getting married?" George asked.

"They haven't set a date yet but maybe we need to set one before you leave. We will talk to them tomorrow. George, would you like to stay here for the night? It's been a long day and we are all very tired," Cindy asked.

"I don't want to put you out, Mom, as you have a full house already," said George, "but I am very tired."

"We will make up the sofa and you can sleep here. It opens up into a full bed so you will be comfortable."

Lynda gave him a couple of pillows and a blanket. "There, I hope it is comfortable," she said.

"It's fine, Mom, thank you." They took each other's hands, as they usually do before they say good night and prayed that everyone would be fine for a while.

"Goodnight Dad and Mom."

"Goodnight son," they said.

The following day, George got together with the boys at the school with Hope and Pete. He thought that they made such a good pair and he was happy for them. George was glad to see the boys and Pastor Olsen. The boys were excited to see George.

"Are you going to stay, George?" asked Jerry. "We can use the extra help."

"Well, only for a little while and then I am returning to the Army to help the men get well and the little children who are sick and homeless."

"Why?" asked Scott.

Hope was listening and she didn't know that he was going back. "George," said Hope, "did you say that you are going back in the Army?"

Pete heard Hope and went by her side to listen to George. "When?"

"Well, since everyone is here and is ready for prayer, I will tell you all. Since I was in the Army, I saw a lot of things that a person should never see."

"Like what?" Hope asked George.

"Soldiers laying on the streets, sick and hungry and hurt, so they had to suffer so much and praying that they could see their family again and little ones without a Mom and Dad to take care of them. They need our help, don't you think so?" replied George.

It was so quiet for a few minutes until Pastor

Olsen said, "I think that George is very blessed to be called to duty a second time. You wouldn't want your friend or family starving would you?"

"When did you know this, George?" asked Hope. You didn't say anything last night. How long are you going to be home?" she asked.

"Well, Hope, if you and Pete set your wedding day, I will be there."

The boys and staff clapped out loud. "Yay!"

They were all surprised because no one knew about the wedding. "How did you know, George?" she asked. Pete and Hope looked at each other. "We haven't set a day yet, bro."

"Well, you better get going soon as I have four months before I need to return. Sis, Pete, congratulations," and then everyone clapped for Hope and Pete.

"Well, I think it's time for a prayer and a song with everyone," said Pastor Olsen.

"George, are you going to help coach?" asked John.

"Well tonight I will be there, but right now I need to go and see someone who needs his Dad right now, and then I need to go see the Davis family, but I will be back." George left to go pick up his son to take him over to see Anna and his grandpa Arthur. He wasn't sure how they would take it, but he had to tell them about returning to the Army. When he got by Cindy's, he picked up little George and gave him a big squeeze and a kiss on his cheek then tickled his tummy as little George laughed and hugged his Daddy. "Let's go see Grandma Lynda okay?"

Lynda was in the kitchen trying to get the dishes done. "Hi, Grams," said George. "How are you? Here, let me help you with them." George finished the dishes and he and the little guy were ready to go by Anna's. "Grams, where is Mom and Dad?"

"They went to church, George."

"Are you alright by yourself?" he asked.

"I will be fine, son, you have a nice visit with the Davis'," she replied.

"Thanks, Grams, we will be back for supper."

"Bye bye," said Lynda and went to read a book and rest for a while. It was mid afternoon and Peter and Cindy would soon be home, so she wouldn't be alone for too long. She was glad that George had stopped by and helped her with the dishes because little Georgie was a handful for her.

George and little Georgie knocked on Anna's

door and Arthur opened it. "I am so glad to see you George, hi little guy," as he said hi to his grandson.

"How is my big guy doing?" and he gave them both a big hug.

"Come on in, Anna is in the parlor. She will be so glad to see the both of you. We sure have missed you both."

"Anna," Arthur called, "come and see who is here. It is George and our grandson."

Anna came out of the parlor and embraced them both with tears running down her cheeks. "I, I am so sorry but Jenny is not here," Anna said.

"Anna!" said Arthur, "you know where Jenny is. I'm sorry, George."

"That's alright, Arthur, I understand," said George.

Anna took little Georgie into the kitchen for some cookies and milk while George and Arthur talked things over. "Arthur," said George, "would it help if I stay here for a few days, maybe Anna and I can look at the pictures, and little Georgie will keep her mind off of Jenny. I told Grams that I would be back for supper but then I can come back. I have to talk to the both of you tomorrow but for now, we will just visit and let Anna see her grandson. How has she been Arthur?"

"She has been very quiet and thinks of Jenny all the time. She doesn't go out very much anymore."

"Can I talk to her Arthur?" asked George. "Maybe if we talk about it, it might help."

"Sure George, you can try."

George and Art went in the kitchen to get little Georgie. Art took little Georgie for a walk to see some of the kittens while George and Anna sat and talked.

"Anna," said George, "how are you? It is so good to see you. I know you miss Jenny and I do too. Anna, do you remember all the people you and Jenny met at the church? How would you like to go and see them tomorrow? We can pick up Cindy and little Georgie and then stop for lunch. How does that sound?"

"I, I guess it would be nice," said Anna. "George? I really miss my daughter and I know you do also."

"I do Anna, I miss her a lot, but God gives us strength to move on with our lives. Although we will never forget the ones we love, God gives us ways of thinking of one who needs help and care.

Anna, will you go with us to the church? Mom will be glad to have you there. Arthur is welcome too as it will be a get-together. Would you like to look at the wedding pictures?"

"I would love to, maybe we can all look at them together. Let's go get Art and little G."

George was very happy that Anna wanted to do it together as a family. The four of them looked at pictures most of the night. Little G fell asleep on Grandma Anna's lap.

So Arthur asked George if he wanted to stay there for the night. "If we aren't putting you out," said George.

"Oh no!" said Arthur, "we had fixed up the room for you and Jenny before all of this happened. We would be glad to have you both stay as long as you like."

"Thank you Arthur and Anna," said George. "Little G and I would be glad to stay. Mom and Dad have a house full right now. Hope is back home for a while until she gets stronger and Grams isn't doing great, so we would be glad to stay with the two of you. Thank you."

"What happened to Hope?" asked Anna.

"I thought you knew?" replied George. "She was in the hospital for a while, but she is back to work and Lynda is just getting older and lame so Mom has her hands full. There is something else that you should know."

"What is it?" asked Arthur.

"Maybe we should wait until the morning." George didn't want to say anything at this time.

"Alright," they agreed and carried little G to bed where his mother used to sleep. "Will this bother you, George? Being in Jenny's room?"

"No, it brings back memories but good ones," he said. "Your grandson and I will be just fine." He gave her a hug and said goodnight to the both of them, hoping that they would sleep better. He decided to call his Mom and let them know that he was staying by the Davis's for the night.

"That's fine George, how are they doing?"

"They weren't too good when I got here, but we talked about Jenny and looked at some pictures and they really enjoyed it. They even were able to laugh a little. I think it helped them a lot Mom with us being here."

"I'm glad George, will we see you tomorrow, George?" asked Cindy.

"Oh sure, Mom, I will be at the school and little G will stay with the Davis'. They get along very well and they love having someone to talk to and care for."

"Did you tell them about rejoining the service and about Hope?"

"No, Mom, I will tell them in the morning."

"Okay, Son, will see you tomorrow then." She thought that her and Peter should stop over and see them tomorrow when George tells them the news. She discussed it with Peter and that's what they would like to do. It would make it easier for George also.

The following morning before they all went to the school, Cindy and Peter stopped by the Davis family. As they gathered for coffee, George held little G on his lap and broke the silence. "Anna, Arthur..."

"What is it George?" not knowing what he was going to say.

"Well, I have enlisted for another four years."

"You did what?" said Anna. "What about little G. Why would you do that?" Anna was very upset with George.

"Anna," said Arthur, "calm down, it's George's decision."

"Anna," said Peter, "we're also surprised, but God has called him to do what he has to do. It is God's calling to help all of the hurt and lost ones that need help. Don't you see, it is George's decision to go and help those who need prayers and comfort. Anna, there is one more thing that might make you happy."

"What is that?" she asked. "I don't want George to leave."

"Anna, Hope is getting married."

Anna dried her eyes and smiled. "That's wonderful. When?"

"Well, George will be home for four months so we need to talk to Hope and Pete. They want George to be the best man, so it will have to be soon. So you see, Anna, you and I have a lot to do to get ready."

"Alright, oh and Cindy, do you want me to help?"

"Of course I do, I couldn't do it without you Anna."

"Thank you, Cindy, I will be happy to help you with the wedding."

"Well," said Peter, "we need to talk with Hope and Pete and set a date. She doesn't know about George enlisting, so after we get home tonight we will talk to them and call you. We need to go now, but we will call you both and let you know."

"Grams will you be alright?" George asked Anna. "Little G can play with the younger boys at the school. He had changed his mind."

"Sure George, we will see you tonight, bye for now."

"Bye Anna and Arthur," replied Cindy. "We will see you tomorrow," as they all left for the school including little G.

Wedding Bells

The following day was a day that they sat and decided on a date for the wedding. They wanted Grandma Lynda to be part of it also. It was a glorious time planning for it. Pete and Hope suggested the 2nd of September. They would have to plan on Pete's Mom and Dad coming and where they would stay.

Since George was going back into the service, he wouldn't be using the house that Peter and Cindy called home, so Cindy asked George, "George, I know that we fixed up the house for you and Jenny, but would you mind if Pete and Hope make their home there? Pete's Mom and Dad could stay with Pete while they are here."

"Mom, it will be our wedding gift to them to call home." He was glad that he could do that for his sister as she means the world to him.

They talked for hours of who was going to be the flower girl, and of course George would be the best man. There was a lot of planning to do and still keep up with the school and the church activities. Hope was so excited, and George was happy for her and Pete. They only had two months to get things ready. It was early June, so they had time to send invitations out and Anna and the two Watkins ladies went looking for a wedding gown. Hope tried several gowns on and finally found one that she liked.

"Mom, look at this one. It is beautiful. Grams do you like it?"

She wanted to include her grandmother because she didn't know how long she would have her.

"It looks wonderful on you Hope," said Lynda. "You will make a beautiful bride dear."

"Thanks Grams," said Hope. "I hope it won't bother George to see it and remind him of Jenny and his special day."

"It will be alright dear. He will love it as he loves you." The four ladies were getting tired of walking around, and were glad that Hope had found a wedding dress.

"Now, don't let Pete see it," said Anna.

Getting ready for the wedding was exciting to Lynda and the family. When Cindy, Hope, and Lynda got home, they were so tired out. Anna had gone home to see how Arthur was, only to find Arthur, George, and Pete had gone and done a little shopping. They had gone searching for a hall to have the dance in. George hadn't had a dance because there wasn't enough time, but they wanted the best for Hope. They found one at the V.F.W. Club. George was able to get it for a small price. It was a nice hall. The band was a band that the church had for all of their doings, and it was a very nice reliable band. Weeks passed and everything had come together.

The following week, Pete's parents were to arrive. When Pete's parents arrived, Pete met them at the hotel and stayed with them until the following day. He drove them over to meet Hope and her parents, and Pete's Mom was amazed at the house.

"How beautiful their house is," she said. "Do you stay here son?"

"No Mom, this is Hope's parents' house. Grandma Lynda lives with them. She is quite old, but a very sweet lady. She's not too well, Mom, but she is sure excited about the wedding. Hope lives here until we get married, and then we will live at her house."

"What do you mean, Hope lives here Peter?"

"She has been in the hospital and they didn't want her to live alone for a while," answered Pete.

"I am staying at her place until the wedding."

"And then what Pete?" asked Pete's Mom.

"Mom, when we are married, we will live in the house that her mother and father got for their wedding gift from Grandma Lynda and her husband George, who died a few years ago."

"Well here we are," said Pete, and walked his Mom and Dad to the door and then the Watkins welcomed them to come inside.

"Pete, come in please."

"Peter, this is my mother and father from Alabama. Hope has met them several times back home when we were in school."

"Welcome Mr. & Mrs. Shilling. We are just settling down for dinner, would you like to join us?" Peter asked.

"We would love to, is Hope home?" they asked.

"No, she has a church meeting with the choir, but she will be home later."

They discussed the wedding at length and

George would of course be the best man. John and Jerry would be groomsmen.

"George or Pete, do either of you know who Hope has for the bridesmaid and maid of honor?"

"No Mom, she will have to let you know when she comes home," George said.

"Oh, Anna, would you like to give a bridal shower or do you want me to," asked Cindy.

"Why don't we do it all together at the church hall," replied Anna.

"That's a great idea," they all replied.

Peter and the other two men sat and listened.

"Why don't we men go on the patio and talk while the ladies discuss the shower."

George and Pete along with the rest of the guys left to get to know Pete's Dad, Mr. Shilling. The Watkins and the Shillings got along very well with each other. Peter showed them their home and introduced them to Grandma Lynda. She was happy to meet them, but was so anxious to see Hope and Pete get married. It was getting a little late and the families were wondering when Hope would be home, and then she finally showed up.

"Hello everyone," as she was surprised to see them all here. "It is good to see you all here. What's the big occasion?" asked Hope.

"Just getting to know Pete's Mom and Dad," replied Peter. "Come on in and I guess you know them."

"I do! It is so good to see you again Mr. Shilling," said Hope. "It has been a long time. Did you ever think that Pete and I would see each other again, and let alone get married?"

"No dear," Mrs. Shilling said, "after Pete left for service, I didn't hear from you."

"Well," Hope said, "you will be a part of our family now and we will see you often, right Pete?"

"You bet," Pete said and told Hope that her Mom had a question for her.

"Well Hope," said Cindy, "do you have the bridesmaid and the maid of honor picked out?"

"Mom, I don't know I haven't asked anyone yet."

"Can you let us know by next weekend, dear?"

"I think so, I need to ask them first but Mom, little George will be the ring bearer, is that okay?" Hope asked George.

"It sure is, he will love it, thank you Sis."

The night was getting late, so the Shillings asked Pete to give them a ride home. The Davis's were also getting ready to go, so they all left at the same time and wished everyone a good night. Hope kissed Pete goodbye and said, "I will see you tomorrow."

When everyone was gone, Cindy and Peter told Hope that she was going to make a beautiful bride.

"You sure are," replied George.

The weeks passed and the ladies of the families got everyone to the church for the shower. They told Hope to meet them there at two o'clock. She had picked out her girls for bridesmaids and maid of honor. Hope met them in the lobby and they told her that someone wanted to see her. As they led her to the main hall, she looked in and everyone said "Surprise!" Hope was very surprised and she shed tears of joy and hugged her Mom and Grandma. When the shower was over, they served a lunch and congratulated Hope. She was a happy girl.

"I want to thank everyone here. It was a wonderful shower and I will see you all at the wedding," said Hope.

Hope had gotten so many gifts. She shed tears of joy. "Where am I going to put all of these wonderful things, these beautiful gifts?"

"Mom, Dad, thank you! Grams, thank you so much. I love you all."

She also thanked Anna and Mrs. Shillings. They all helped to clean up and helped Hope carry her gifts home. Pete hadn't been there because he had school duties. He had taken over Hope's place for a while, but how Hope was back. She was preparing for the big day. Cindy, Anna, and Mrs. Shilling were busy decorating the hall on the morning of the wedding. Hope was busy with Lynda and getting her dressed special. Grandma Lynda meant the world to Hope and she was the Grandma that she had and loved her dearly.

George and Peter were dressing in another area where memories came back to George. He wasn't sure that he could do this and he thought of Jenny.

"Dad, I, I can't do this, I'm sorry."

"George!" said Peter, "son, you have to do it. Hope's counting on you. You can't let her down now."

"I'm sorry, I can't and he ran out of the room and outside."

There were only a few minutes before the bells would chime for the signal. The church was full and decorated with beautiful flowers along the pews. Little George was so exited and he asked Pete, "where is my Daddy?"

"He will be back, Little G. He had to step outside for a while."

"For what?" asked little G, "I want to go by my Daddy."

"Let's go and find Grandma Davis."

Peter took him over by Jenny's Mom and Pete, and Peter went to find George. George had been sitting outside the church when Peter found him. George had been praying and asking God why?

"George," said Peter, "are you alright?"

"Son, I know that this has been very hard on you after losing Jenny."

"I, I didn't think that it was going to bring back memories like this."

"But they are good memories George. Aren't they?" asked Peter.

"Yes Dad, I'm sorry."

"Well, I think they are waiting for us inside. Come on, let's go in and see your sister get married today, okay?"

Pete had taken George's hand and the three of them walked in the church together. As they walked in, the guest clapped their hands and George and Pete waited until the rest of the bridal party walked down the aisle. Watching little George walk down the aisle put a smile on

George's face, it made him think of how much Jenny would love to see her son all dressed up in a suit.

When the others were all in, the bridal song began to play, and Peter and Hope walked arm in arm as they reached Pete and Peter kissed his daughter. While putting her hands in Pete's, Peter walked back to sit with Cindy.

"What happened?" asked Cindy, "is George alright?"

"He will be, dear, he just had a few bad minutes and he didn't think that he could do it but he is okay now. He loves Hope and he wouldn't do anything to hurt her."

As Pastor Olsen gave the speech, George and Hope smiled at each other. It was like they could read each other's minds, then Pastor Olson asked for the rings. Little George gave him the rings and George was so proud of his son.

Pastor Olson asked Pete the usual question, "do you Pete, take Hope, to be your wedded wife until death do you part?"

George looked at Hope as Pete turned to her and said "I do." Hope then was asked the same question and answered "I do."

Then, forgetting to ask who gives the bride to

be wed, the Pastor asked the question and Cindy and Peter said "we do."

Pete and Hope clasped hands and the Pastor replied: "You may now kiss the bride."

The happy couple walked out to start their lives together and pictures were taken of the couple and the proud parents together. The reception was held in the hall down in the church and no alcohol was being served.

"The cake is beautiful," said Hope.

She didn't want to cut it, but she knew that they had to after dinner was over. Hope and Pete were so happy. It was a whole new life for them. When dinner was served, George stood and gave his best man speech.

"Hope. Pete. We want to congratulate you both and pray that you will always have a beautiful life together, and always honor each other. Your lives have taken you to a new crossroad and, and…" he started to choke up a little bit as he was thinking of the road that he and Jenny had taken.

Then Peter stood up realizing that it was hard for George to do. So, he continued. "Thank you George as that was a wonderful speech. Hope, Pete, we, Cindy and I and Lynda, hope that God will always keep you both safe and happy, and we are very proud to be your parents, and some dreams are swept along the deep sea," said Peter.

"Some are lifted up to the sky, but never give up on the dreams that you can't see. But through it all, count your blessings and remember, God is only a prayer away and never give up on your dream."

"Thank you George and Dad as that was a beautiful speech."

Then the bells started clanging which meant kiss each other. Then they cleared away the tables and the dance began, first the bride and groom, and then George and Hope danced while Pete danced with his mother, and then Peter, Hope's Dad, danced with Hope. He was so proud of his daughter.

"You are still my little girl Hope. You and George are my pride and joy."

Tears began running down his cheeks while dancing the waltz.

"Now my young lady, I think your husband is waiting for you," as he put Hope's hand in Pete's hand. After the crowd left, and Hope and Pete said their goodbyes, and then George asked them, "where are you going for you honeymoon?"

"Well George," said Hope, "we are going to

wait until you return to service. That way we can spend more time with you and little G."

"Oh no," said George. "You go and have a good trip. I have a month to go yet, so you will be able to go while I help Dad keep the school running. When you return, we will have a family get together, just you and I, okay Hope? I love you Sis." They hugged each other and said goodbye.

They really hadn't made any plans, but George and Peter had handed them two envelopes before they left, but Pete hadn't opened it until they got in the car and was so surprised to see two tickets to the Holy Land.

"Wow," he said, "Hope, look it," Pete was so excited.

"What is it Pete?" Hope asked as Pete handed her the large envelopes with the tickets in them. Hope's eyes sparkled with joy.

"So now, we have plans to make Pete," she said, "but not until next week."

She wanted to thank everyone who gave them this opportunity to go and see this beautiful site that they had never seen. They were so happy.

"We have wonderful parents," said Hope and Pete.

"We couldn't have done it without all of them and George," said Pete.

They couldn't imagine the joy and blessings that they had received. They called Peter and the rest of the family and thanked them for the wonderful gift.

The next few days were busy days for Hope and Pete as they were getting ready for the big trip called their honeymoon. This was going to be a honeymoon that they would never forget, and they will definitely need their cameras.

"There will be so many places and things to see."

"There sure will be," said Hope, "and Mom and Dad will love to see the pictures."

"Pete, God has given us so many blessings and I know that our lives will be forever filled with love and happiness, don't you?"

"I sure do Hope, my darling. We are going to have a good life together and we will have two sets of parents to help us."

They finished packing and wanted to see the families before they left that afternoon. So they went by Peter's folks' first to say goodbye, and hugged them and then said, "thank you Mom and Dad Shilling, we love you."

"Where are you going now?" asked Pete's Dad.

"Well, we are going to see Peter and Cindy, Dad, to say goodbye to them. We will send you a postcard alright," said Pete.

"Okay, son, have a great honeymoon."

Meanwhile, Cindy, Peter, and George were visiting with Lynda as they wanted to spend as much free time with her as possible. As Hope and Pete walked in, it was quiet so they both called out, "hello, is anyone home?"

"In here kids," Cindy said. "Come on in."

"Hi Mom and Dad, is everything alright?" they asked.

"Oh yes dear, we were just visiting with you Grandma and talking about the wedding and how happy we are for the two of you."

"George," said Hope, "are you sure that you don't have to leave until we get back?"

"No, it's all good Hope, everything will be okay, and I will still be here when the two of you return."

"Alright George," said Hope.

"Hey bro, would you mind driving us to the airport," she asked.

"Sure, I would be glad to, when are you guys

leaving?" he asked.

"Very soon," Pete replied. "In about thirty minutes but we wanted to see everyone and thank you all for the wonderful gifts, and Grandma, thank you also," and Hope gave her a big hug.

"I love you Grandma."

"I love you too sweetheart, and you have a safe trip and God bless you."

Hope kissed her Mom and Dad and Pete shook hands with Peter.

"Okay George, we are ready to go now."

"We love you all," said Hope as they left.

"You have a good time," said Peter. "See you when you get home."

As they left, Peter turned to Cindy and said, "I love our children, but...but."

"What?" asked Cindy

"...but," said Peter, "it sure is nice and quiet."

Peter held Cindy in his arms and said, "let's go rest by the fire and just enjoy each other's company now that our twins are grown up, we can spend more time with Mom."

"Okay dear, but we will have George and little G to worry about. I sure wished that he hadn't joined the service again as I will miss him."

"Yes dear, I do too but this is what God has called him to do. He will be home once in a while on a leave so let's make him happy while he is home now. George and I will take good care of the boys and you can watch Mom, okay?"

"Yes Peter," said Cindy, "but what about the children's choir at the church?"

"They will have to substitute one for two weeks," replied Peter, "and we will talk to them tomorrow."

They sat quietly by the fire and were ready for the Bible prayer, and when they finished they checked on Lynda and called it a night. Little G had stayed by Grandma Anna, and George went there after he took Hope and Pete to the airport.

It was pretty quiet at the boys school the next morning when George and Peter got there. The kids were waiting for Hope arrive and to hear her music.

"Good morning boys," said Peter.

"Good morning, Peter," said the boys.

"Where is Hope and Pete? We don't have any music," said Scott.

"Hey Scott," said George, "you can play the piano and the boys can all sing along, can you do that?"

"I, I guess I can," said Scott, "what do I play?" he asked.

"Any song that Hope and Pete taught you to sing," replied Peter.

Scott picked out a couple of the songs that they all knew. Songs like "Jesus Loves Me" and "Give Thanks".

"That's wonderful Scott," George and Peter said, and then the pastor and the boys said their morning prayer before breakfast. It felt so good to Peter and George to be working together.

"It has been nice, son, remember when we were always here and you were the coach? I can't wait until you get out of the Army, son. We will miss you a lot."

"I will miss you too Dad and Mom, but I will be home on a pass in a few months, and little G will be at a special Christian school also."

"When do you have to leave, son?" asked Peter while driving to the church.

"I have to leave when Hope and Pete get home, about two weeks after that, Dad. We will all get together and watch or look at their wedding pictures and listen to the stories of their honeymoon and Anna and Arthur can come over along with the Shillings, and then you and Hope can maybe go riding or do lunch together. I know that she is happy, Dad, but when I see them together, it makes me think of Jenny and how happy we were together. I really miss her, Dad."

"I am so sorry George but someday you will find someone else."

They arrived at the church and met the staff members so they could let them know that Hope couldn't be there for two weeks, and then they went home to find Cindy putting supper on the table. George stayed for supper and talked to Grams for a little while, and then he left to go and see his son before bedtime. George stayed with the Davis's to let them know how much he cared and missed Jenny.

Hope and Pete were gone on their honeymoon, Peter and George were busy at the school, as it was a peaceful and quiet week for all of them. The Shillings were getting ready to head back to Alabama. The time was going so fast, and they enjoyed their time with all of the families. As they finished packing and getting ready to go, they called Peter and asked if he would take them to the airport.

"Are you going home?" asked Peter.

"Yes, we need to get back home to take care of things."

"Sure, we can help you with that. What time does your plane leave?" asked Peter.

"Well, we are ready to go now, is that alright?" asked Mr. Shilling. "Our plane leaves in two hours."

"Okay, we will be over soon."

He had to let George know, and then he would pick up Cindy and Lynda. He wanted to take them for a ride. When he got home, Cindy asked what was wrong.

"Nothing dear," said Peter. "I thought that you and Mom would like to take a ride to the airport when I take Pete's Mom and Dad there to catch their plane home."

"We would love that, did they let Pete know that they were leaving?"

"I don't know, dear, I'm sure they did," Peter said.

As they drove to the airport and waited for Mr. & Mrs. Shilling's plane, they had a lot to talk about, and said that they had a very nice time.

"You have a very nice daughter, and I know that Pete will make her very happy," said Mr. Shilling.

"Thank you both for coming, it was nice

meeting the two of you," said Cindy and Lynda. "We are family now so we will keep in touch and you do the same, okay?"

"We sure will, but we must go now, so give Pete and Hope our love, and we did let Pete know that we were leaving today."

"That's good," replied Cindy. "Well the both of you have a safe trip back home."

As they parted for the plane, Peter and Cindy watched and waved goodbye until they couldn't see the plane anymore.

"What a nice couple," said Peter. "Pete has very nice parents, doesn't he?"

"They are very sweet dear," and then Cindy turned to Peter and said, "you are too dear" and he smiled.

The week passed and Hope and Pete had returned from their honeymoon. They had taken many pictures of their honeymoon. When they got to their house, they were glad to be home. Worn out from walking and tired, they sat and relaxed for a while then they decided that they would let the unpacking go until the morning, so they called it a night and said a prayer together as Peter has always done. They would call their folks in the morning when they wake up.

As a new day dawned for them, Hope called her Mom and Dad to let them know that they were home safe.

"Hello, Mom, Pete are I are home now, so we thought you would like to come over and see the pictures."

"We would love to, did you have a good trip Mrs. Shilling?" asked Cindy.

"Mom, we did but I am still a Watkins okay? I guess I need to get used to the name now. When do you want to come over?" Hope asked. "How is Grandma and George?"

"They are alright dear, your Dad and I will see you tonight after work, okay?" It will be good to see the both of you. We will let George and the Davis's know, alright?"

When the day ended, they all gathered to look at the pictures of their honeymoon and welcomed the newlyweds home.

"It was a happy and wonderful trip, Mom and Dad. We want to thank all of you folks as we couldn't have done it without you all, and we brought you all home something."

They handed each one a picture of them in a little church that Hope and Pete had attended in the Holy Land.

"These are wonderful kids. I love them," said Peter and Jenny's parents.

"We have one for my folks also," said Pete. "We are sorry that we didn't get to see them off though. Thank you for taking them to the airport, Peter."

"You are welcome Pete. We were glad to do it. They are very nice people."

George was very quiet as he looked at the pictures. Pete looked at him and said, "George, are you alright?"

"I, I'm sorry if the pictures are too much for you," Pete said, "but we can see them at another time if you'd like."

"No, no, that's alright, I have to get used to it," said George. "They are wonderful pictures and you and Hope should treasure them always."

"Thank you George," Hope said, "we sure will."

The night was getting late and George said that he had to go but he reminded Hope that the two of them would get together in a couple of days. Cindy and Pete hugged the children and said goodbye, and that her children are all grown up now.

"Mom, we will always be your children and if ever you need us, we will be there," Hope and

George replied. "We love you!"

"We love you too," replied Peter. "We better get Lynda home now. See you all tomorrow," she said. As everyone left, Hope and Pete sat and looked at the pictures some more and would always treasure them.

George kept his word, and called Hope the following Friday.

"Hope, are you able to spend the day together? We have a lot to talk about."

"Sure George, I'm looking forward to spending time with you. I always enjoy your company after all, we are twins. Bro, do you have to go back to the service?"

"Yes Sis, it is God's calling, but I will come and pick you up in half an hour, okay?"

The two of them went to lunch and talked about the days growing up together and how Grandma Watkins played outside with them after school.

"George," said Hope, sad but trying to keep her tears back, "I miss Grandpa a lot and I really love him."

"I miss him too, Sis, but he is happy in heaven and we can talk to him at anytime and he will hear us."

"Grandma misses him too, she talks about him a lot," replied Hope.

"Well soon she will see him, Sis, and then they will have each other forever. She isn't very well, is she, Hope?"

"No, George, if anything happens to her, would you be able to come home?" asked Hope.

"You bet I will," George said. "Our family is very precious to us. Well, what do you say we go and see some old friends?"

"That would be nice," said Hope.

They visited many of the friends that they grew up with, but it was starting to get late. They stopped at the park next to the house that was a place called home for the whole family.

"Sis, the house that you and Pete are living in will be a place called home for our family. We have all been blessed by Grandma and Grandpa."

"Yes, George, Mom and Dad are always going to love this house. It is their wedding gift from Grandma and Grandpa," replied Hope. "George, I guess we better get back home as I have a church choir to go to."

"This has been great spending time together, Sis. I will keep in touch with all of you alright?"

"I hope you do George because Mom and

Dad worry a lot when you are gone."

They went back and Hope said to George, "I will never forget our time together today, George."

"It has been so wonderful don't you think so?"

"Yes ma'am, and I will miss the entire family, but you have Pete now to watch over you Sis, but please always watch over Mom and Dad and Grams."

"I will bro," replied Hope as they went their separate ways.

"I will see you tomorrow," George said.

As George returned to Anna and Arthur's place, he stopped to see how little George was as it would only be another week before he had to leave, so he told Anna and Arthur that he was going to spend the last week over by his Mom and Dad's place. So, they sat up quite late and talked about all the things that happened, and how God had gotten them through all of it.

When morning came, George got his son ready to go by Cindy's to visit his grandparents. It would be a while before he would see them again. First he stopped at the school to see the boys and to listen to Hope play her music. He had taken a recorder with him so he could listen to it while he was away.

He was sure some of the boys would enjoy that. Little George got to know the boys and had fun playing with them. George was ready to leave but little G wasn't ready just yet.

"Dad, can I stay with Pete and Aunt Hope? Please, Daddy?"

"Well, we need to ask them if it's okay with them," said George.

"Can I, Auntie Hope? Can I stay?" little G said.

"Sure you can," she said. "I can bring him home when we are done George. I would love to have him here with us."

"I guess it's alright son but you do what they tell you to do, okay?"

"I will, Daddy, I love you."

George left to spend some time with his Mom and Dad. As he arrived home, he entered with a loud, "hello? Is anyone home?" With his luggage in his hands, he sat them down and Peter and Cindy greeted him with open arms.

"We are glad to have you for at least a few days, son." Cindy smiled and George gave her a big hug.

"Where is Grandma?" he asked.

"She is sitting in the family room watching a movie," said Peter.

"Come on in, where is little G?"

"He wanted to stay by the school and play with the boys so Hope and Pete will be bringing him over later tonight."

They walked into the family room where Lynda was trying to watch TV, but had fallen asleep. "Grandma," said George, "Grams." But Lynda didn't answer so George shook her a little bit and she finally woke up.

"Grandma, are you alright? This is George."

Lynda looked at him, not knowing who it was.

"I, I saw an angel, she was a beautiful angel."

"Mom," said George, "what does that mean, Dad? Did you call the doctor?"

"No, she said, she didn't want one. She said that she is tired, so let's get her to bed and see if she will eat some soup first."

But Lynda didn't want any. Cindy had called the doctor after getting Lynda into her bed. Peter and George waited for the doctor while Cindy sat beside her until the doctor arrived. Dr. Johnson arrived and checked Lynda over and then went to talk with all of them in the other room.

"What is it Dr. Johnson?" asked George.

He was very concerned about Lynda.

"Well, I am sorry to tell you but it is her heart. She is having a very hard time breathing tonight. Peter, may I talk to you alone?" said Dr. Johnson.

"What is it Dr. Johnson? You can tell all of us," they replied.

"Okay," said Dr. Johnson. "I have to prepare you all for tomorrow because she may not make it through the night."

Hope and Pete had come home and heard what the doctor said.

"Oh no!" Hope cried out. "She can't go, please, please, help her!"

"I, I can't dear," said the doctor. "Her heart is very weak and it's working really hard my dear. I am so sorry Hope as he took her in his arms to comfort her."

"Peter, keep a close eye on her tonight and if you need me, please don't be afraid to call me, alright? Please, just remember all of the good times that you had with her and the joy that you gave to her life."

Little G was puzzled with all of the tears and commotion that was happening. He went by his Dad and wanted him to hold him, not knowing what was wrong. George had taken his son and got him ready for bed.

"Daddy?" said Little G. "Will you read me a story, please?"

"Sure little one, what about the lost sheep? Is that okay?"

"Yes, Dad," as he curled up under his blanket and with his soft bear that Grandma Lynda had given him. He had loved his Grandma Lynda with all of his heart. While George read Little G a story, little G fell asleep. The four of them took turns staying by Grandma's side. They all prayed over her and remembered times when Grandpa was sick. Hope was pretty young then, but she remembered when she got to sit on his lap and he gave her and George a horsey back ride. She remembered enjoying her time with Lynda also, playing games and laughing together.

"Hope? Do you believe in angels?"

"Yes, Mom, why?"

"Well, Grams said that she saw an angel today. She always said that that was her sign, that God would call her home."

In Cindy's mind, Lynda was her mother because Cindy's mother Mary died shortly after she and Peter were married. As they took turns, Hope stayed by her bed all night as she couldn't leave her Grandma's side as she looked at Lynda early in the morning and called Peter to come into Lynda's room. As they all came in by Hope, they knew that she was gone, but had called Dr. Johnson and he had come right over. As Dr. Johnson examined Lynda, he told them that she was gone and then Peter and Dr. Johnson had gone out of the room to talk with each other. Dr. Johnson had signed the death certificate for them and shook hands with Peter.

"I'm very sorry Peter," he said as he left.

They all shed tears for Lynda and said, "God she is in your hands now, please take good care of her and we love her and miss her a lot."

Pete took Hope in his arms and told her, "It's alright dear ,as she is in a beautiful place now."

The services were at the church where many of the members attended.

"It was a wonderful service," Rev. Olsen replied.

There were a lot of people who showed up, and some spoke of memories that they had of Lynda. For Peter and Cindy, she was the most precious mother anyone could ever want. Peter went back to the time when Lynda and George Sr. found him and adopted him as a Watkins, and made him a member of their own family. John and Jerry also gave their condolences. They loved Lynda too, just like she was their own Grandma.

A week later, George had to say goodbye, but because of Grandma Lynda's passing, he took more time from the Army to stay and help his Mom and Dad get things in order. It had been a hard thing to lose Lynda, Peter's adopted mother. He would always remember her and George Sr.. George and Little G stayed with his Mom and Dad but would visit Anna, Jenny's Mom and Dad, before they had to leave to return to the Army.

"Son," said Peter, "when do you have to go back to the base? Can you stay another week? We can really use your help."

"Yes, Dad, I called the Army and I told them the situation and they gave me another week, so whatever you need help with, Dad, I will be here to help you, alright?"

"Thank you Son, that will be very helpful of you and there is a lot to take care of."

Along with keeping the school going, Peter and the family had Lynda's cemetery stone and many of her things to take care of. Peter and Cindy along with Hope couldn't bear to go into Lynda's bedroom and not find her there without shedding tears. She meant more to Peter than anyone could imagine.

"Dad, are you alright?" asked George as he noticed how sad Peter looked.

Cindy looked up at Peter and put her arms around him, knowing how much his mother meant to him.

"I will be fine, Son, it's just the thought of not seeing her that makes it hard, but God has called her to rest now."

The Watkins family was a praying family, and no one could doubt their love for each other or for God. Cindy and Hope finished going through Lynda's clothes and personal things. Lynda had written in her Bible that it should go to Hope, and Hope was so glad to receive it. It would always be something to remember her Grandma by.

"Pete will love this, Mom."

They continue sorting things out, and Peter and George went to the school to check on Pete who was helping John and Jerry with the boys. Then came a new boy, very hostile and he didn't want to stay at the school. His parents couldn't handle him at home anymore.

As Peter walked in by Pete, he said, "what is going on, Pete? Who is this young boy?"

John and Jerry were trying to calm the young lad down and couldn't, and even his parents had tried but couldn't get through to him. Peter walked over by the parents to talk to them.

"Hello," he said, "I am Peter Watkins, I run the school. How may I help you and the boy?"

"Hello," said Mr. and Mrs. Barton. "We are David's parents and we have had a hard time this last year with him. He is so defiant and won't do anything, and he won't even go to school. We thought that maybe being with other boys might help him. He needs a lot of discipline."

Peter and the parents talked and signed the boy into the school.

"Come," said Peter and he and George told Pete also to follow them to see where David's room would be because Pete and Hope were soon going to be in charge while George was gone. John and Jerry introduced David to the other boys, but David didn't care who they were. He hated his parents for doing this to him. When Mr. and Mrs. Barton left Peter's office, Peter called David in to talk with him. David's parents walked over by him and said, "We love you son but we believe that this is the best thing for you."

"You mean for you," said David.

"For all of us," replied David's Dad.

Peter told the Bartons that it would be better

if they didn't see David for a few days as it would help David get used to the boys and staff here at the school.

"Alright," said the Bartons, "we will wait for your call to let us know when we can come and see him."

"Peter, he isn't a bad boy," said David's Mom, "and we do love him with all our hearts."

"We will do the best we can," said Peter. "We have had some very unhappy boys before."

They said goodbye to David and asked him to please be good during his time at the school. Peter asked Pete to come into his office with him and David so that Pete would have the chance to get to know David.

"Sit down," Peter said, "I would like to talk to you. I hope you will like it here, David. this guy standing here is one of the staff members. He is my son-in-law and he is a very nice guy so can you shake hands with him?"

David just looked at Pete and didn't say anything even though Pete had put out his hand to him.

"Okay," said Pete, "what happened between you and your parents?"

"Why do you have to know?" asked David.

He wasn't about to tell them or talk with them. He was so angry at them.

"David, we want to help you, but if you don't feel like talking, we will let you stay in your room for today until supper. Would you like to be alone, David?" asked Pete.

"Yes, just leave me alone," said David.

Pete took David to his room and said, "when you feel like talking, we will come and get you, alright?"

David looked around his room as he was surprised how nice it was, but he didn't mind being alone. As he looked around, he saw some of the pictures on the walls and he took the pictures down and set them on his dresser. He knew who it was in the pictures because he used to go to Sunday school and church, but his parents wouldn't go with him. This is part of the reason that David is rebelling against them and he thinks why should he have to go to church if they won't go.

Meanwhile, the three Watkins men talked with John and Jerry to see if they could get David interested in baseball or whatever David would like to do.

"We will be glad to try Peter," they said, "but

we can't promise anything right now as he is new to the school."

"Please, just do your best," asked Peter.

As the afternoon went on, David came out to talk with George and Peter.

"Well, we are glad to see you out of your room," they said. "What would you like to do, son?" Pete asked.

"I would like to talk with Mr. Watkins," David said.

"Sure, David, come on let's go for a little walk."

Peter and David walked outside and looked at the grounds.

"Wow," said David, "you have everything here: basketball, soccer, and even a yard for the younger boys."

"The boys all have things that they like to do, so we try to make it the best we can. We even have a football team in the fall but you are a little small yet for that. How about we go in and meet some of the boys?"

"I would like that, sir," David said.

"Do they have their own room too?"

"Not all of them do David, because like you, they need to get used to the other boys that are here first."

Peter and David got along really well until Peter asked him about his parents and why he was so angry with them.

"Can you tell me, son?" asked Peter.

"I love my Mom and Dad, Mr. Watkins, but they never spend time with me or go to church with me. Why can't they do things together? "

"Well, David, we will talk to them again and maybe we can help you, but let's go join the boys in the school."

As they walked back in the room, David had a smile on his face.

"Wow," Pete and the other staff said.

"What did you say to David, Peter? He is all smiles."

"Well, David and I had a very nice walk and talked about different things, didn't we, David?"

Peter introduced him to a group of boys his age. David was twelve years old. At that age, life is very confusing. As the evening came and it was time for Peter and George to leave, Peter said to David and the other boys, "see you all tomorrow."

He stopped and talked to Pete, "maybe you can give David a little extra attention tonight before you leave, he could use a good ear to listen to."

"I will, Dad," Pete said, surprising Peter. "I hope you don't mind me calling you Dad," said Pete.

"No, I am just surprised, that's all. I would be honored to have you call me Dad like Hope does."

"Well, I will see you at home because Hope has been with her Mom today helping to get things organized, so see you later son," and they both smiled at each other.

The following week came too fast for George. Little G enjoyed being at the school with the other boys but now, he would have to say goodbye, as well as George does also. George was to leave the following day to report back to the base. He was excited about going, but didn't want to leave his Mom and Dad alone. He knew that his sister Hope would be fine with her new husband, Pete.

George Returns to Service

As George was preparing to leave for the service, Cindy was preparing a get-together for his goodbye. She had gotten John and Jerry, Hope and Pete, and all the boys and staff members together for a farewell party. She wanted it to be a great day that he would always remember. Hope and Pete got the boys choir together to sing "America the Beautiful" and some other songs that George liked. They even thought about little G. He would be going also, and they would miss them as much as George and his son would miss being home. Peter and Cindy called Anna and Arthur to come over and join the party also.

The day had come and George wanted to leave early so he didn't miss their flight.

"Are you ready to drive us to the airport, Dad?

Little G and I are ready to go now."

"Yes, son, but wait, I want to see if Cindy is ready to go also. Dear, George is ready to leave now."

"Alright, I'm ready," as she walked out wiping her eyes, dreading to see her son leave again.

"Mom, you are crying," said George. "Please Mom, don't cry, I will be alright and so will little G. We will write or call you, I promise, Mom."

"I am okay George, I just don't want you to go," said Cindy.

"I will be home before you know it, Mom."

"Well you two, come on, we need to go."

"Come on little G, Grandpa will carry you."

They all got into the car and Peter drove to the school.

"Dad, are we stopping at the school?" asked George.

"Yes, son, only for a little while to say goodbye."

When they arrived at the school, the boys and the staff were all waiting for them.

"Hi George and Mr. Watkins," they yelled.

"Hi boys," he replied. "This is a surprise. Thank you."

Then he saw Hope and Pete. He walked over by them and Hope said, "Bro, the boys have a song that they want to sing for you."

He smiled and he and the family sat down to listen to it, and then Hope and Pete sang "Wings on a Dove."

"That was wonderful, Hope. You and Pete are a good pair."

"Thank you, George," she said.

Georgie said to his Dad, "can you say goodbye to Auntie Hope and Uncle Pete?" Little G ran to Hope and put his arms around Hope and Pete.

"I love you," little G said.

George turned to the boys and said, "you sang very well, I will always remember you all."

"Son," said Peter, "we have a record for you to take with you. It's one that the boys and your sister recorded so you would have something to listen to when you need to hear our voices."

"Thanks, Dad and Mom, I will cherish it always, thank you Hope and Pete also. Well, I must go now, so you all take care and remember that God is only a prayer away."

Cindy, Peter, and Hope rode to the airport with George and little G to see them off. They would miss the two of them. When they arrived at the airport, they all hugged and cried and told George to remember that God is always with them. As George was leaving, Peter said, "Wait son, I have something I want to give to you that you can carry in your pocket."

"What is it, Dad?" George asked.

Peter handed him a piece of paper to George and smiled.

"This will comfort you when you are helping others in need. I love you son," and Cindy hugged him and also said, "I love you too, son."

"I love you, Mom, Dad," replied George and gave Hope one last hug and said "I love you Sis."

"I love you too, bro, bye," as George and little G walked out of sight, the three of them watched as they boarded the plane and were waving to them until the plane was out of sight.

As they returned home, they were all three pretty quiet.

"Dad," said Hope, "what did you give to George?"

"It was a poem dear I had gotten it from another pastor. It was a beautiful verse. I remember getting one when I was a young boy in Sunday school."

"You still have it, Dad?"

"Yes, Hope, it was something that I treasured for all of these years and now I thought that it was time to give it to George while he was so far away from us."

"What did it say dear?" asked Cindy. They were all very curious.

Meanwhile, George and his son were settled on the plane. Little G had fallen asleep but George was curious as to what his Dad had given him, so he took it out of his pocket and started to read it.

"The Cross in My Pocket"

I carry a cross in my pocket
A simple reminder to me
Of the fact that I am a Christian
No matter where I may be

When I put my hand in my pocket
To bring out my wallet or keys
The cross is there to remind me
Of the price he paid for me

It's also peace and comfort I share
With all who know my master

And give themselves to his care

So, I carry a cross in my pocket
Reminding no one but me
That Jesus Christ is Lord of my life
If only I'll let him be

When George finished reading the verses, he put it in his pocket and thought how comforting it had made him feel.

Now that everything had calmed down, Peter and Cindy had decided to retire and put the school in Pete and Hope's charge until George would be home. Lynda was gone and their son George had gone back to serve his country. Hope and Pete were happily married now. It was time that they spent some time together.

Peter asked Cindy, "why don't you and I go on a trip together? We haven't done that for a long time."

"That is a great idea dear, I really think we should. We will make plans next week and let the children know."

"Where would you like to go?" Peter asked.

"Well, we haven't seen Mike for a while, and then I thought that we could just travel until we are ready to come home, maybe Texas, Colorado or California," said Cindy.

"Well, I suppose we could but that will take a lot of gas money and hotel cost and food, but we really deserve this darling, don't you think so?"

"You bet I do," Peter said.

"Well then, let's do it. The school is in good hands with Hope and Pete."

"Yes," said Peter, John and Jerry can help also.

They took hands and embraced each other. "This is going to be wonderful. Let's go and talk to Pete and Hope." Cindy called the kids and told them that they were going to stop by the house and talk with them.

"Mom, Dad," said Hope, "what's wrong? Is everything alright?"

"Yes dear, everything is just fine," replied Peter.

"Then what is it?" Hope asked.

"Will you and Pete be able to take care of the school while your Mom and I go on vacation?"

"Dad, I think that's a great idea. You and mother haven't been on a vacation for a long time and the two of you deserve one.

"We will do just fine while you are gone," replied Pete. "We have a good staff and John and Jerry will help us out."

"Are you sure that you are going to be okay?" asked Cindy.

"Sure, Mom, Pete is here for me now so you go and have fun but before you go, please stop at the school, alright?"

"We will, dear, we are retiring when we come back and leaving the school in your care, Hope."

Peter and Cindy packed their suitcases and were ready to leave in the morning. "Well, sweetheart, are you ready to leave on our long trip?" asked Peter.

"Oh yes, dear, I am so excited to go and see the world and all of God's beauty."

They drove off looking back at the house to make sure that they didn't forget something. Then they stopped at the school to say goodbye to Hope and their new son-in-law.

"Where are you two going?" Pete and Hope asked. "How can we get in touch with you if we need you?"

"We are going to see Mike first, do you remember Mike? I told you about him," said Peter.

"Yes, Dad, I remember him, then where?" Hope asked.

"Well, we are not too sure dear, but we will call

you wherever we go, okay?"

"Thanks, Mom and Dad, we love you," said Pete and Hope. "Thanks for trusting us with the school."

"Well, someday, it will be yours and George's when he gets home," replied Peter.

"How long will you be gone? We are not sure, about three to four weeks unless you need us sooner," replied Cindy as they gave each other a hug and said goodbye.

"Have a good trip, Mom and Dad."

"We will, dear. Goodbye."

Cindy and Peter stopped to see Mike, the young lad that they picked up on the street. Mike had grown into a nice young boy and was happy to see the Watkins again.

"Mr. Watkins, I'm glad to see you and Mrs. Watkins again."

"Well, we are glad to see you too, Mike. How are you, Mike?" asked Peter.

"Fine, I love my parents and they adopted me just like you, Mr. Watkins," replied Mike. "What are you doing here?"

"Well, Cindy and I are on our vacation, so we thought that we would stop by and see you. Then we are on our way to wherever our car takes us, so maybe we will see you on the way back, alright?"

"I hope so," said Mike.

"Well, we must go now, Mike. You are looking so good, take care okay? We love you," said Cindy.

"I love you too, Peter and Cindy, bye and have a safe trip." Mike was so surprised to see his friends that had helped him when he was a young boy who was hungry, homeless and living on the streets.

Peter and Cindy traveled to Colorado, Kentucky, and then California and enjoyed every bit of it. They visited zoos and the museums of art. On weekends, they would stay in a hotel and attend church on Sundays. The last week of their trip was a trip to Disneyland. They had never seen it or been there, so they decided to stop and visit Mickey and friends. They felt young at heart and didn't want to go home.

The last week of their travels, they stopped at Mike's, and then spent the day with him. Mike was doing so well. The following day, they were on their way home and were very tired but they enjoyed their trip very much.

"Where did the month go, Peter?" Cindy asked.

"I don't know darling but we sure had a good trip.

I loved going to the gratos to see the seven steps of where Jesus was crucified, didn't you dear?"

"Yes, I love it and it was beautiful dear. The kids will love all of the pictures that we took along the way. Wouldn't it be nice to return and go wherever we wanted, even stop to see George?" Cindy asked.

"It would be great if they took over the school, but I'm not sure that they are ready to take over yet. Let's give them another year or so, so they can get adjusted to the idea," Peter replied.

"That's a good idea. What about the church?" Cindy asked.

"Oh, I will always be there as long as they need me."

When they returned home, Pete and Hope met them and had a good dinner cooked for them.

"Hi Mom and Dad," they called out. "How was your trip? We are glad to see you back home safe and sound."

"Well, we had a wonderful trip. We saw so much and took so many pictures."

"Are the two of you hungry?" Hope said.

"We sure are," replied Peter. "We didn't stop to eat."

"Well, come on, have a seat, Dad. Dinner is all

done and ready to eat."

"Wow," said Cindy, "you two are wonderful."

"These steaks look so good. Well, let's eat before they get cold."

They all sat down and Peter said grace. They talked about the trip and all the pictures that they had taken and how they stopped to see Mike.

"Who is Mike?" Pete asked.

"He's a young boy that we picked up on the side of the road. He didn't have clean clothes or any food to eat. He had run away from his foster parents whom Mike didn't like," explained Peter.

"Is he alright now, Dad?"

"Yes, son, he is very happy and has new parents now, and they love him with all their hearts," said Peter.

They discussed the school and how things were good and that John and Jerry were very helpful.

"That brings your mother and I to this question," Peter said.

"What is it, Dad?" they asked curiously.

"Well, your mother and I have been talking about retiring from the school next year, and we thought that you two would like to take it over for us."

"Are you positive, Mom? Dad?"

"Yes dear, we think that it is time that you two and George when he comes home would be the sole owners of the Christian School for Boys. Your father and I will always be there for you, if you need our help."

"We will always need your help, Dad, when we get a troubled boy in and you know that we won't let you down."

"You also have George and Pete to help you," said Peter and Cindy.

"Oh, Dad, we can do it, Pete and I along with John and Jerry and when George gets home, he can be in charge. He's good with the boys when he's coaching. We will be just fine, won't we, Pete?" asked Hope.

"Yes, sure we will. I am new at it, but I have two good in-laws for parents. You have helped me a lot, Dad."

"Well, you have helped us a lot also, Pete, especially when Hope was sick, you were there for her."

"I love her, Dad, and I will always take care of her."

"We will check in every once in a while to see if you are okay," replied Cindy. "So, let's just plan on one year from today."

"Okay," said Hope.

"We will be fine," replied Pete and Hope.

"God will always be there for the two of you."

The decision was made and the date was planned for October 1st. It would be a beautiful fall day. After talking and setting a time and looking at pictures, Hope said, "well, I think we will let you two get some rest after the long trip."

Peter Retires

Hope and Pete were busy with their music and the boys. David, the new boy had become very nice and cooperated with the staff. He was getting along with the other boys too. Hope kept her practice at church and Sunday choir. Things were going well for all of the families.

The year passed quickly for the whole family. Peter and Cindy went to the church often to see the members and visit shut-ins. When the end of September came, Hope and Pete had called George.

"George, can you come home in October?"

"Why, Hope, he asked, is there something wrong?"

"Nothing is wrong, but Mom and Dad are going to retire at that time and we want to have a retirement party for them. Can you make it?"

"I will try, Hope. Hey sis, what are you doing for them?"

"We have made a plate for them to honor Grandma and Grandpa Watkins and their son Peter Watkins for starting the boys school and the many years that they have taken troubled boys in and have taught them with loving hearts to always help others."

"That's wonderful sis, I will see you next weekend. I love you sis," replied George.

The week passed and Hope had sent out invitations to friends and church members. George had come home for the weekend as he would not have missed the special Moment that his Mom and Dad were going to have. He was to give the speech for the big day and he had stayed by Hope and Peter's place. In the morning, they called Peter and Cindy and asked them to come to the school for a little while.

"We will be there this afternoon dear, alright?" said Cindy. They met them at the school where many people were sitting waiting for them. As they walked in, everyone stood up and clapped.

"Well, what is this Hope?" asked Peter and Cindy. George, "I didn't know that you were home, "Cindy said as Peter gave him a hug and Cindy shed tears as George said "congratulations."

"This is a surprise George, I, we, your father and I didn't expect a big going," said Cindy, "who's idea was this?"

"Mother, Hope and Pete called me after you got back from vacation and we planned to do it together."

"Peter!" Called out a voice from the crowd, "we don't want you to retire," yelled David Barton, the new boy. "No, we don't," shouted another voice, which was Scott.

Hope and the pastor asked Peter and Cindy to please make a speech for everyone, so he did.

"Hello everyone, it is quite a surprise to see so many friends and all the boys here. As you have heard, Cindy and I are retiring and we are leaving the school in my three children's hands. you know all three of them. They have done a very good job while we were gone, so I know that they will be fine running the school without us. I do ask that you all honor them as you have my father George Sr. and I. We are very proud of our school as many boys would not have had a home if my father and mother Watkins hadn't opened it up. I will always be around if anyone needs Cindy or I. Thank you all for coming and I will keep in touch with all of you."

"Peter," said Pastor Olson, "Hope and George have something that the school would like to present to you and Cindy."

"Alright, Hope and George," said Peter.

Hope and George stood up and Peter and Cindy waited on the platform while Pete walked up to reveal what was covered up. All three uncovered the large plate to put on the outside of the school. Peter could hardly believe his eyes, "how did you all do this?"

Cindy cried, "oh my, this is wonderful."

The boys and the crowd stood and gave them a standing ovation and then they sang: "You can't be a beacon if your light don't shine."

"It is beautiful, thank you all. It is something that we have always wanted to get and I know my father and mother are looking in on all of this, thank you again kids and all of you boys and friends."

"Dad," said George, "we will all remember Grandma and Grandpa Watkins."

"This school was started by two of the most giving and loving people who love children and cares for everyone with all of their hearts. Helping lost children was their one priority. Dad, we want to dedicate this plate to your parents, Mr. George

Sr. and Lynda Watkins, and to you and mother."

As the crowd gave another standing ovation. Peter and Cindy were so proud that they were speechless, but were able to find the words "thank you son and Hope and to you to Pete and to all of you here. We are so proud to have received this gift, but it will be for everyone to remember how much the school and this town had meant to my father and mother, thank you."

"It is beautiful and I know that your Grandma and grandpa are looking in on all of us," said Peter to the twins.

The plate had a beautiful cross on the top of it with the words reading: To George Sr. and Lynda Watkins and family for the dedication that they have given to this school and town.

"We present to you, Dad," said the children as they all stood and Hope and Pete led them in the lovely song: "You can't be a beacon if your light don't shine" and the crowd joined in.

Well, Peter and his family did shine their light on all the people and now Hope, George and Pete, would carry on the family tradition. The Christian School for Boys would always live on for boys who needed a place called home. The Watkins are very proud of their heritage and their children, for it would live on forever. God had returned to them all that they could expect which was joy, love, and happiness.

About the Author

I was born in Wisconsin in 1932 and placed in an orphanage for 3 years. I then moved to a farm where I grew up and enjoyed all the animals. I loved feeding them and walking in the fields.

My great-grandfather was the founder of the famous Pillsbury Mills in Minnesota in the 1800's. After graduating from Waupaca High School, I moved to the town of Waukesha, WI. I married in 1954 and have three birth children, and adopted a baby girl who is as precious as my birth ones. Her name is Karen.

I love going for walks and helping other people. I enjoy the Joy Circle Group at church and have been a member of the First United Methodist Church since 1957. In Waukesha, WI, writing my book, A Father's Love, has made my faith in God strong enough to get through life a lot easier.

www.ingramcontent.com/pod-product-compliance
Lightning Source LLC
Chambersburg PA
CBHW071205090426
42736CB00014B/2721